CW01582510

Frank Worth

'A Collection Discovered'

Written by Austin and Howard Mutti-Mewse.
Introduction by Nicholas Shoolingin-Jordan.

Edited by Kate Courtenay

Text © Cinemage Limited 2002 & TBS.Inc
(Turner Broadcast Systems Incorporated)

Colour photographs restored by Richard Hadley
Black and white photographs printed by Melvin Cambetti-Davis

Printed by Offset Colour Print Limited
159 - 179 Empress Road, Southampton, Hampshire, SO14 OJW
Telephone: 023 8063 2111 Fax: 023 8063 0033

Cover Photograph of Marilyn Monroe by Frank Worth (1954)
© Frank Worth/Cinemage Ltd. 2002

Layout and Design by Lee Denvir of TCM (Turner Classic Movies)
© TBS Inc. All rights reserved

The authors would like to thank the following individuals for their contribution to 'Worth Exposing Hollywood': Judith Allen, Pamela Blake, Mary Brian, Grace Bradley Boyd, Ben Campbell, Hilda Campbell-Russell, Bill Cappello, Alex Carruthers, Kirsty Craik, Shannon Davis, Jean Dean, Lee Denvir, Ann Dunne, Joe Dunne, Muriel Evans, Flare Media Communications, Mette Haack, Nick Hart, Mary Henely, Rose Hobart, Joy Hodges Schiess, Joanna Gabb, Adam James, Georgie Lloyd-Parry, Joan Marion, Dorothy Mackaill, June MacCloy, Mae Madison, Addie McPhail Sheldon, Joan Marsh, Anita Page, Margaret Pellegrini, Gene Raymond, Leisel Revett, Beverly Roberts, Ann Rosen, Patricia Russell-Exner, Miriam Seegar Whelan, Janet Shoolingin-Jordan, Peter Shoolingin-Jordan, Mildred Shay Steele, Jill St. John, Lupita Tovar Kohner, Sara Vaughan, Helen Williams, Sarah Wise, Jane Withers and Grace Wong.

Our very special thanks go to Michael G. Riley

All photographs in this publication are © Frank Worth/Cinemage Ltd. 2002

All rights reserved. No part of this publication may be reproduced or transmitted in any shape or form or by any means, electronic or mechanical, including photocopying, recording, or information storage or retrieval system without the permission in writing from Cinemage Limited, London

Published by Cinemage Limited
19 South Audley Street
London, England
W1K 2NU
www.cinemage.co.uk
Telephone & Fax: +44 (0) 20 7491 0807

A CIP catalogue record for this book is available from the British Library

ISBN: 0-9543703-0-9

For more information on Frank Worth's touring exhibition and to order prints and other fine art merchandise, please visit www.frankworth.com

Worth Exposing Hollywood

"Frank Worth was a man of character and taste. He had a keen eye for beauty and a remarkable talent for translating that beauty onto film. All of us who were photographed by Frank owe him a huge debt."

Mamie Van Doren
(2002)

TCM
TURNER CLASSIC MOVIES

TCM (Turner Classic Movies) is unmissable movies 24 hours a day from Brando to Redford, Bacall to Sinatra, Garland to Eastwood. Available on cable and satellite TV. www.tcmonline.co.uk

A DIAMOND IS FOREVER

Cinemage would also like to thank following sponsors: Abbey Well, Admirable Crichton, The Athenaeum Hotel, The Berners Street Hotel, Chivars Regal, Cool Glow, Daniel Undhammar, 51, Buckingham Gate, The Four Seasons Hotel, Ice Box, Kosmopol, The Meridien Hotel, NBA (Neilson, Bainbridge & Artcare), Pölstar, Robert Bullock Furniture and Works of Art, Sunjuice, The Hempel Hotel, Vale Wedding Cars Ltd and William Alexander Wines.

hp invent

CHILDREN'S WISH FOUNDATION INTERNATIONAL

ABOUT THE AUTHORS

Austin and Howard Mutti-Mewse

Identical twin brothers, Austin and Howard Mutti-Mewse, harbour a mutual passion for cinema that dates back to their early childhood.

Born in Weybridge, Surrey in 1972, they were raised on a diet of black and white movies. This fascination made way for written correspondence with many of Hollywood's film legends, including Lillian Gish, James Stewart, Marlene Dietrich and Bette Davis.

In June 1993, an exhibition of their collected ephemera was held at The Museum Of The Moving Image (MOMI) in London. The Daily Telegraph hailed it, 'A must for all fans of the cinema.' That same year, the brothers visited California and met with some of their ancient pen pals for the first time. Subsequent trips to the USA followed and a decision was made to record these former actor's stories on film.

Following the completion of their Bachelor of Arts degree in graphic design, Austin and Howard have been diligently working to raise finance for this documentary, *I Used To Be In Pictures.* A chance meeting with Barbara Broccoli, daughter of the late 'James Bond' producer Albert 'Cubby' Broccoli, has fortuitously helped the brothers to realise the project. Both Austin and Howard live in London and independently work as freelance journalists for broadsheet newspapers, magazines and film websites.

CONTENTS

INTRODUCTION

An Extraordinary Discovery

Los Angeles, December 2000. Following his death, the family of penniless 'Reluctant Genius' Frank Worth cleared through his dusty and muddled possessions. They came across a series of incredible photographs, many of legendary Hollywood stars. His relatives knew that he'd been friends with the likes of James Dean and Marilyn Monroe, and that he'd also earned his living as an often-uncredited freelance photographer. But what they then discovered in his jumbled apartment, was a remarkable photograph collection more precious than could ever have been anticipated.

There were more than 10,000 black and white and colour photographs, the majority of which were unpublished. Frank Worth had recorded a personal and unique history of the last golden era of Hollywood.

The Collection

The collection consists of some outstanding images from Elizabeth Taylor's first wedding to the infamous shot of Marilyn Monroe with her dress blowing up, taken late one evening on location in New York for the film 'The Seven Year Itch' (1955). The photo of Marilyn includes director Billy Wilder and was taken seconds before the News Syndicate photographer's famous shot. Frank only released his photo many years later, for a one-off publication in Variety, part of a featured tribute to Billy Wilder.

The majority of the photographs in the collection are from in the nostalgic era of the 1940s and '50s. Significantly, since Frank Worth was a close friend to many of the stars, his pictures capture something very different to those of his contemporaries. Below are just some of the screen legends featured:

James Dean
Gregory Peck
Jayne Mansfield
Barbara Stanwyck
Ava Gardner
Joan Crawford
Rock Hudson
Doris Day
Natalie Wood

Clark Gable
Elizabeth Taylor
Frank Sinatra
Grace Kelly
Groucho Marx
Humphrey Bogart
Betty Garrett
Russ Tamblyn
Ginger Rogers

Lauren Bacall
Cary Grant
Bette Davis
Errol Flynn
Sammy Davis Jr.
Marilyn Monroe
Ann Miller
Fred Astaire
Abbott & Costello

A COLLECTION DISCOVERED

Even in photography circles, Frank Worth is barely known. He eked out a modest living as a freelance photographer in Hollywood during the nostalgic 1940s and '50s. At this time most photographers were tightly controlled by the constraints of a powerful studio system. However, with his close personal contacts, Worth sidestepped these restrictions and captured images that would never normally have seen the light of day.

Later on in his life, it appears that Worth would not allow anyone - not even his close family - near the photographs he regarded as his private album. After his death however, the Worth family felt that recognition was well overdue. It now looks as if Frank Worth, the artist, is set to posthumously become as iconic a figure as those he photographed.

FRANK WORTH

Frank Worth was born in New York City on March 23 1923. In 1939, as a junior at Erasmus High School in Brooklyn, he joined the college photographic club. During his senior year he approached the New York offices of the International News Service (INS) with some of his images and was hired. His first assignment was to photograph movie stars as they stepped off the California Express train in New York's Central Station. This was his introduction to the people of Hollywood. Frank was charming and witty and immediately struck up a rapport with his subjects. As a result, the INS sent him to Hollywood as a staff reporter when he graduated. He soon became a member of the Hollywood Photographers Guild and quit INS although continuing to work for them on a freelance basis.

Once in California, Frank met and became close friends with James Dean and, because of a mutual love of fast cars, was invited on the sets of 'Rebel Without a Cause' (1955) and 'Giant' (1956). Infact, Frank was often invited to visit many important film sets including 'Sunset Boulevard' (1950), 'How To Marry a Millionaire' (1953) and 'The Seven Year Itch' (1955). He also attended and photographed a number of Oscar and Golden Globe ceremonies as well as the after-parties. Worth came back with variety of amazingly candid shots of the likes of The Marx Brothers, Errol Flynn and Joan Crawford.

Frank Sinatra arrived in Hollywood a couple of years after Worth and they gravitated towards the same places, becoming close friends. Through Sinatra, Frank met Rat Pack regulars, Dean Martin and Jerry Lewis. The latter even had a part in Frank Worth's unfinished film, 'The Silent Treatment' (1967), a movie that featured many of his famous movie pals.

One of the most important aspects of Frank Worth's private and professional life was his enjuring friendship with Marilyn Monroe. Years before her debut in the 'The Asphalt Jungle' (1950) - the movie that launched the legend - he'd taken many photographs of the young starlet. History relates that Worth was actually the first photographer to have snapped the infamous "Blown white skirt" shots in New York. Pictures from the shoot were never published due to studio objections over the amount of underwear on show! Consequently, it was re-staged later on in Los Angeles, which meant it was opened to news syndicate photographers. Interestingly, Worth regarded many of his images to be as intensely private as his own personal life. For instance, he only admitted to a long-standing affair with Monroe just months before his death.

When Frank's beloved baseball team, the Brooklyn Dodgers moved to LA in 1959, their delighted fan saw his big chance for a career move. Infact he became the team photographer and remained involved with them until his death. During this time he also became a major contributor to The Sporting News, completing about thirty covers a year, up to the 1980s.

Frank Worth died in Los Angeles in December 2000.

KINGS OF COMEDY

BOB HOPE

The greatest American comedian of his day, Bob Hope became America's richest entertainer - a far cry from his poverty stricken childhood in Eltham, London. After some years on the stage as a dancer and comic, he made his first film appearance in 'The Big Broadcast of 1938' singing, 'Thanks for the Memory' - his signature tune. One of Hope's most successful films of the period was his own re-tailoring of the horror spoof 'The Cat and the Canary' (1939). His career spanned nearly fifty movies (ending in the late 1980s), with perhaps most memorably, the infamous partnership with Bing Crosby and Dorothy Lamour in the 'Road to...' comedies (1940-52). During WWII and the Korean and Vietnam Wars, he spent much time entertaining the troops in the field. For these activities and for continued contributions to the industry, Hope was honoured with five Academy Awards, the Kennedy Honours Life Time Achievement Award, and amongst many others, a 1998 honorary knighthood. The most popular entertainer of Western civilisation celebrated his ninety-ninth birthday on May 31st 2002, in the company of his wife Dolores, at their home in Toluca Lake, California.

Top Three Films:
'The Cat and the Canary' (1939)
'Road to Singapore' (1940)
'Road to Rio' (1947)

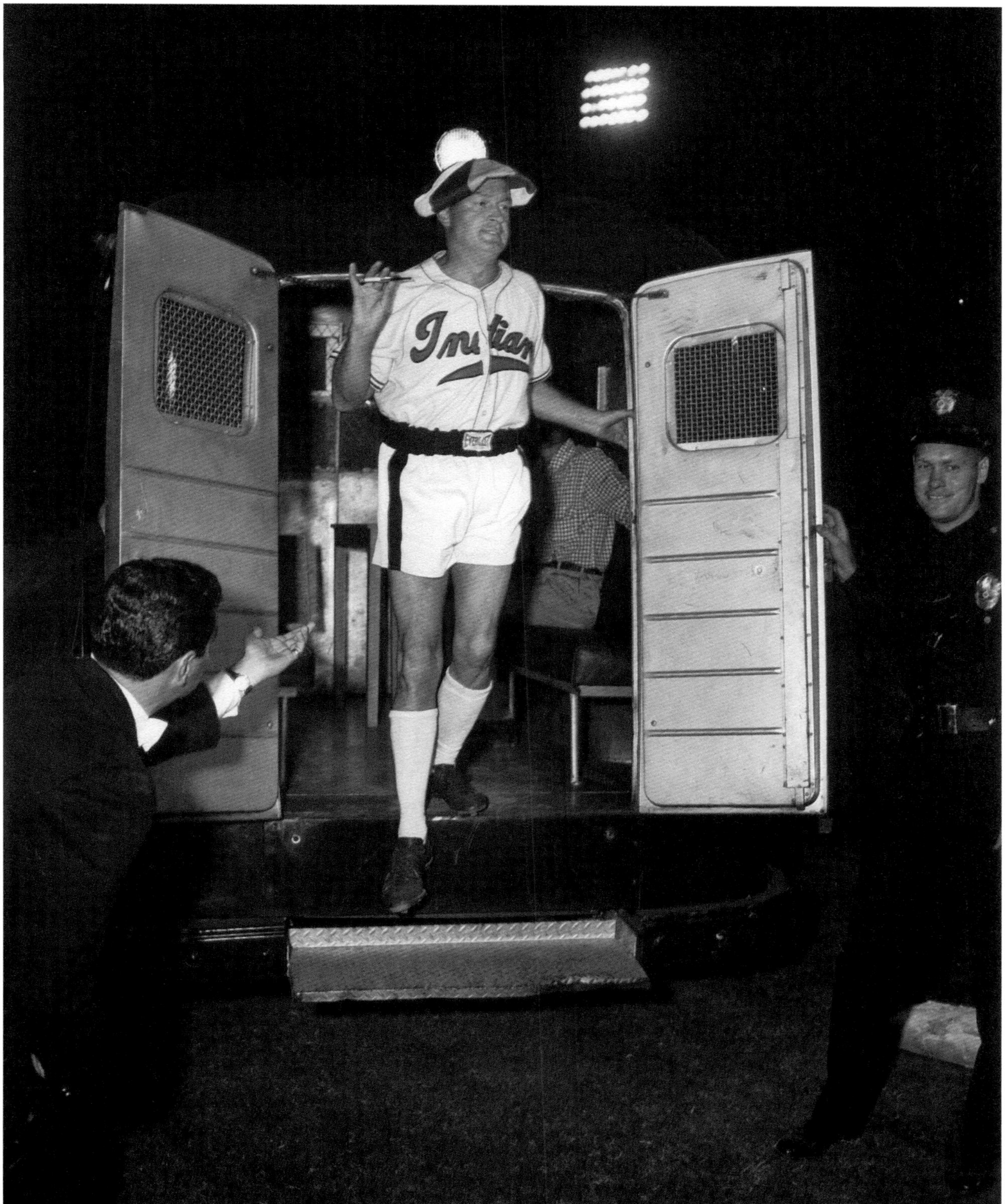

BOB HOPE CHOOSES HIS OWN UNIQUE STYLE OF TRANSPORT

GEORGE JESSEL

Actor, producer, composer, writer, comedian and Hollywood confidant, George Jessel ventured into show business, aged eleven, much to the disgust of his strict Jewish family. Before long, he had joined forces with Eddie Cantor and was performing in vaudeville shows. He entered movies in 1919, playing Evelyn Brent's brother, Davy Simon, in 'Another Man's Wife' and continued to act for a further seven decades, seldom receiving parts worthy of his extraordinary talent. In 1945, 20th Century-Fox successfully signed him as a producer. He was formerly married to the actress, Norma Talmadge. Jessel died 1981.

Top Three Films:
'Love, Live and Laugh' (1929)
'Stage Door Canteen' (1943)
'The George Jessel Show' (1953/4)

GROUCHO MARX

It was Sammy Davis Jr. who best summed up Groucho when he said, *'There's Groucho, then there's all the rest'*. Groucho Marx was the first of five brothers to start a stage career, eventually being joined in the early 1920s by Chico and Harpo for the musical comedy, 'I'll Say She Is'. This occasion marked another 'first'. Groucho's infamous moustache and fat cigar, and Harpo's curly wig and harp, later all became trademarks of the Marx Brothers. They became cinema's best-loved comedy act. Groucho, who in later life enjoyed a solo career, went on to appear in over forty pictures in fifty years. June MacCloy worked with Groucho, Harpo and Chico on 'Go West' (1940). *'Oh it was a big deal for me to be in a Marx Brothers movie,'* she recalled in August 2002. *'The Brothers were fun, but oh boy, were those movies exhausting to make'*. Apart from a huge following in the movies, Groucho was also known for being a liberal, and on occasion making controversial political remarks. These subsequently led to an investigation by the FBI, who believed him to be a communist. His biggest solo success was the 1947 radio comedy quiz show, 'You Bet Your Life', which made its transition to television in 1950. In 1974, Groucho received an Honorary Oscar for the Marx Brothers' contribution to motion pictures. He died in 1977.

Top Three Films:
'Animal Crackers' (1930)
'Duck Soup' (1933)
'Day at the Races' (1937)

GROUCHO MARX (R), WITH GEORGE JESSEL AT THE BALL GAME

DEAN MARTIN

The 5'10" smooth-talking, hard-drinking Dean Martin was born Dino Paul Crocette in 1917. He was an established nightclub singer before entering into a partnership with comedian Jerry Lewis, rocketing the pair to superstardom. Even without Lewis, Martin was a supreme talent in his own right. One of his best-remembered films was 'Ocean's Eleven' (1960) which teamed him alongside Frank Sinatra, Sammy Davis Jr., Peter Lawford and Joey Bishop - 'The Rat Pack'. He was opened to an even wider audience when he hosted 'The Dean Martin Show' on television (1965-1973). Martin also became a major recording artist with hits like 'Memories are Made of This'. He played all the top nightspots globally, including his favourite haunt, The Sands Casino in Las Vegas. Seldom seen without a cigarette or glass of bourbon, he once quipped, *"Every star needs supporting players"*. He remained a constant figure on the Hollywood scene until his son's tragic death in a plane crash in 1987. After that, he retreated to his Beverly Hills house, passing away on Christmas Day 1995.

Top Three Films:
'Artists and Models' (1954)
'Ocean's Eleven' (1960)
'Robin and the Seven Hoods' (1964)

JERRY LEWIS

Comedian, actor, writer and director – Jerry Lewis' rubber-faced, often juvenile characters earned him a place in entertainment history as one of the greatest physical comics of all time. During the 1950s, the phenomenal Lewis and 'straight man' Dean Martin, ruled supreme - appearing together on television, nightclubs and in seventeen films, before eventually going their own separate ways in 1956. Lewis' first solo film, 'The Delicate Delinquent' (1957), proved he could go-it-alone. His hit movies confirmed him as a hugely bankable star, earning Paramount Pictures a great deal of money. He turned his hand to directing with 'The Bellboy' (1960), after which he made 'The Nutty Professor' (1963), hailed by critics as a movie masterpiece. Off-screen, Lewis was a huge baseball fan, playing with numerous professional teams and training every year with the L.A. Dodgers. Jerry Lewis has become equally renowned for hosting the annual muscular dystrophy telethons and in 1984, was awarded the French Legion of Honor. He lives in California.

Top Three Films:
'Hollywood or Bust' (1956)
'The Bellboy' (1960)
'The Nutty Professor' (1963)

COMEDIANS DEAN MARTIN, JERRY LEWIS AND BOB HOPE IN RARE SOMBRE MOOD

MERVYN LE ROY

One of the most prolific director/producers during the Golden Age of Hollywood, Mervyn Le Roy kept a high profile long after his directing days were over, even attending a screening of 'The Wizard of Oz' (1939) - which he produced - on the eve of his death in 1987. In 1906, when Le Roy was just six years old, the great San Francisco earthquake shook up his father's fortune, leaving the family penniless. Mervyn sold newspapers and entered talent contests in the vain hope of earning a living. Then Le Roy decided to contact his cousin, Jesse Lasky, the company head of 'Famous Players Lasky'. His first job was as an assistant to the wardrobe master at the studio. He moved through the ranks quickly becoming a comedy gag writer and 'bit' part actor in such silent films as 'Ella Cinders' (1926), alongside saucer-eyed flapper Colleen Moore. In the 1930s, he joined First National, a subsidiary of Warner Bros. The studio dubbed him 'The Boy Wonder' after Le Roy started the gritty gangster genre, directing massive blockbusters 'Little Caesar' (1930) and 'Gold Diggers of 1933' (1933). Wearing his producer hat, Le Roy instigated bringing 'The Wizard of Oz' (1939) to the screen. In the 1950s, he set up his own production company making such memorable movies as 'Gypsy' (1962).

Top Three Films:
'Little Caesar' (1930)
'The Wizard of Oz' (producer only) (1939)
'Mister Roberts' (1955)

BARBARA STANWYCK

Most of America's audiences remember Barbara Stanwyck as the matriarchal figure, Victoria Barkley, from the hit television western, 'The Big Valley'. Later she starred in the popular drama series 'The Colby's', but millions of fans will also remember a sparkling movie career spanning from 1927 to 1964. Born Ruby Stevens on July 16 1907, in Brooklyn, New York, Stanwyck went to work at the local telephone company for a mere $14 dollars a week, but she harboured the urge to enter show business. When not working the switchboard, she pounded the pavement in search of dancing jobs. Persistence paid off. Aged seventeen, Barbara was hired as a chorus girl for the princely sum of $40 a week. In 1928, Barbara moved to Hollywood where she was to embark on one of the most lucrative film careers ever seen, cementing the niche of melodramatic bitches and psychotic killers. In 1982, Stanwyck received an honorary Oscar for her contribution to film, an American Film Institute Lifetime Achievement Award followed five years later. She died in January 1990.

Top Three Films:
'Stella Dallas' (1937)
'Double Indemnity' (1944)
'Sorry, Wrong Number' (1948)

BARBARA STANWYCK AND MERVYN LE ROY ARE ENTERTAINED BY GOOFBALL JERRY LEWIS AT CIRO'S

BUD ABBOTT AND LOU COSTELLO

The "straight man" of one of show business' most popular comedy duos, Bud Abbott, spent much of his childhood in the Coney Island section of Brooklyn. There are several versions of how and why the team originally got together. Costello recalled that Abbott filled-in for his regular straight man one night and never left. Abbott's account tells of a first meeting in a burlesque house in upstate New York. In reality, both comics never quite agreed on the beginnings of their famous partnership. They toured in vaudeville and before long, were topping the bill at most venues. Hollywood then called and their first film, 'One Night in the Tropics' (1940) was produced by Universal. Next, the studio starred the team in a low budget comedy, 'Buck Privates' (1941). Its enormous success (grossing $10 million) convinced the studio that Abbott and Costello were there to stay and were, without doubt, bona-fide stars. The pair seldom got on, but no one watching their comedy routines would ever have known it. Costello was a short, fat eccentric. Abbott was thin, dour and easily exasperated. Separate from their movie career, the pair are the only two non-sportsman honoured in the Baseball Hall of Fame in Copperstown, New York for their "Who's on First Base" routine. Famed for their backchat and slapstick, the Abbott and Costello story ended in an acrimonious split in 1957. One year later, Abbott filed suit against Costello for $222,456.19, claiming he was still owed for a television series they had once made together. This was still legally unresolved at the time of Costello's death in 1959. Bud Abbott died fifteen years later in 1974.

Abbott and Costello: Top Three Films:

'Buck Privates' (1941)
'Abbott and Costello Meet Frankenstein' (1948)
'Abbott and Costello in the Foreign Legion' (1950)

COMEDIANS ABBOTT AND COSTELLO SHARE A QUIP

LIBERACE

Born Wladziu Valentino Liberace in 1919, the flamboyant pianist is most fondly remembered for his extravagant costumes, huge gems and trademark sparkling candelabra. His fans adored the unique style that eventually earned him the title of 'Mr Showmanship'. At just four years old, he was playing the piano, with a gift for emulating any tune by ear. The teenager Liberace performed in local theatres and nightspots. After graduating from the Wisconsin College of Music, Liberace then went on to perform in larger venues to capacity crowds. He entered movies in 1950, making his debut as a showy pianist in 'South Sea Sinner' (1950). Two years later he had his own television show. By the 1970s, Liberace was credited as the highest paid musician in the world, paying out an extravagant $100,000 a year on his dazzling, brocaded, diamond and jewel-encrusted costumes. Despite a wonderfully camp image, Liberace successfully sued a London newspaper in 1959, for printing an article insisting he was a homosexual – something he always denied. By the mid 1980s, he was suffering from a heart condition and performing his very last concert in 1986. Tragically Liberace died of the AIDS virus the following year.

Top Three Films:
'Footlight Varieties' (1951)
'Sincerely Yours' (1955)
'Batman': The Dead Ringers/Devil Fingers (tv) (1966)

JIMMY DURANTE

Jimmy Durante, fondly referred to as the old 'schnozzola' (because of his extraordinarily large nose), became the living embodiment of the term 'beloved entertainer'. Born in New York City in 1893, Durante dropped out of school in the eighth grade. Two years later, he played ragtime piano for a living, snapping up jobs wherever he could - in bars, cabarets and whorehouses. For a time, he became known as 'Ragtime Jimmy'. In the 1920s, Durante teamed-up with the dancer, Lou Clayton and singer Eddie Jackson, to form a vaudeville act. By the end of the decade, the trio were performing for the impresario Florenz Ziegfeld on Broadway. Amidst the mayhem that greeted the arrival of talking pictures, Durante saw an opening for himself and persuaded director Hobart Henley to cast him, Clayton and Jackson in 'Roadhouse Nights' (1930). Gripped by a taste for the movies, he then decided to go it alone, playing solo comedian to such actresses as Lupe Velez, Marion Davies and Joan Marsh. *"He was passionate with an effervescent humour,"* said Marsh in 1998. *"Everybody knew Durante. He was really famous, especially for a number of beloved catch phrases including: "It's a catastrophe!" "Surrounded by assassins!" and "Everybody wants ta get inta da act!". Now it seems, like the rest of us, darling Jimmy has been forgotten"*. Durante was at his greatest when performing in front of a live audience and was a regular at the famed 'Friars Club' in Hollywood. His boundless energy ensured a varied array of film roles, many of which were inferior to his natural talent. Jimmy Durante died in 1980.

Top Three Films:
'Palooka' (1934)
'Jumbo' (1962)
'It's a Mad Mad Mad Mad World' (1963)

NO DIAMONDS?! JIMMY DURANTE IS ASTOUNDED AT THE SIGHT OF A SOBER-SUITED LIBERACE

DONALD O'CONNOR

Donald O'Connor is best remembered for his exhilarating role as Cosmo Brown in 'Singin' in the Rain' (1952). Suffering from total exhaustion, he needed three days bed rest after the 'Make 'em Laugh' frenetic musical sequence. O'Connor was just as effective as a comedic lead, playing the cheeky little companion to 'Francis the Talking Mule'. Born into a vaudeville family, O'Connor hit the road as an infant, making his film debut with his siblings in 'Melody for Two' (1937). Paramount signed him the following year and, apart from time spent with the armed forces during WWII, he's been working ever since. Accomplished as a serious composer of classical music, O'Connor has spent recent years conducting the Los Angeles Philharmonic Orchestra. He lives with his second wife, Gloria Noble, in California.

Top Three Films:
'Are You With it?' (1948)
'Francis' (1949)
'Singin' in the Rain' (1952)

DEBBIE REYNOLDS

Debbie Reynolds' first ambition was to be a majorette. Her story rivals that of Cinderella. She was crowned 'Miss Burbank of 1948' at the tender age of thirteen and subsequently was offered a contract by a Warner Bros. talent scout. By 1950, she had moved to MGM. Her big break came a year later, when Gene Kelly requested her as his leading lady for 'Singin' in the Rain' (1952). Playing a chorus girl that dubs for silent movie siren Jean Hagen, her rendition of 'Good Morning' was warmly received by both Kelly and Donald O'Connor. Sassy and full of determination, Reynolds eventually tried to break away from light-hearted musicals, favouring more substantial comedic roles. The transition failed to pay off, with the exception of 'A Catered Affair' (1956). She married singing sensation Eddie Fisher in 1955. Three years later, the marriage ended abruptly when Fisher left Reynolds for the beauteous Elizabeth Taylor. A born survivor, Debbie Reynolds became a treasured figure in Hollywood.

Top Three Films:
'Singin' in the Rain' (1952)
'Tammy and the Bachelor' (1957)
'The Unsinkable Molly Brown' (1964)

DONALD O'CONNOR WATCHES DEBBIE REYNOLDS JUMP FOR JOY

ABBOTT AND COSTELLO

Donna Martell, the dark haired star of Westerns, remembers how the laughter left comedic genuis Lou Costello on the death of his son, Lou junior. Frank Worth had become close to Costello and was the only photographer to shoot father and son together. (Donna Martell spoke to journalist Paul Parla for Classic Images magazine.)

'The first picture I made after I signed with Universal International was 'Abbott & Costello Meet the Killer, Boris Karloff' (1951), and I remember that this was done around the time Lou Costello's infant son died. Lou was a fine person, and he was trying his best to get through it all, but his actions were indeed acting and nothing more. He was not the same person after his son's death: something died in him, and it was apparent to just about everyone who worked with him'

Donna Martell
(1999)

ABBOTT AND COSTELLO, CHAPERONED BY GEORGE JESSEL (L)

JACK LEMMON

Jack Lemmon had his first taste of show business performing voice-overs for radio. He began appearing on television and then on Broadway during the first half of the 1950s, demonstrating his acting ability early on. His role as the irrepressible Ensign Pulver in 'Mister Roberts' (1955), won him a Best Supporting Actor Oscar. It was not, however, until 'Some Like It Hot' (1959) and then 'The Apartment' (1960), that he found his true screen persona - that of a decent man struggling against the world and occasionally succumbing to failure. During the 1960s and 70s, Lemmon received much praise – and deservedly so - for his cinematic partnership with Walter Matthau. They then re-teamed in 1993 for 'Grumpy Old Men'. His second wife was the actress Felicia Farr. Jack Lemmon died of cancer in June 2001.

Top Three Films:
'Mister Roberts' (1955)
'Some Like it Hot' (1959)
'The Apartment' (1960)

ALDO RAY

Aldo Ray, was the archetypal fifties screen 'tough guy', with distinctive looks and a voice that his former wife, Jeff Donnell, said resonated like sandpaper scratching on glass. The son of Italian immigrants, Ray won a scholarship to UC Berkeley before then serving in the US Navy, and fighting in Japan between 1944-46. He was a novice actor when director David Miller gave him a 'bit' part in 'Saturday's Hero' (1951). Ray portrayed an air of vulnerability as a man on the verge of divorce in 'The Marrying Kind' (1952). Later that same year, he played the dim-witted boxer in 'Pat and Mike' (1952), alongside Spencer Tracy and Katharine Hepburn. Ray's extravagant lifestyle forced him to accept dire scripts and film offers far beneath his talents, including a hard-core pornographic film, 'Sweet Sexy Savage' (1982), and the sci-fi horror 'Biohazard' (1985) co-starring Carroll Borland. Aldo Ray died in Martinez, California in March 1991.

Top Three Films:
'The Marrying Kind' (1952)
'Men in War' (1956)
'The Naked and the Dead' (1958)

JACK LEMMON AND ALDO RAY (R), ENJOY THEIR ICE CREAM AT MUSSO AND FRANKS GRILL, HOLLYWOOD

MARLON BRANDO

Marlon Brando, acclaimed by many as the greatest American actor of all time, made his screen debut in 'The Men' (1950). A troubled youth, Brando had been expelled from a number of schools including a military academy. In 1943, Brando arrived in New York and enrolled on a course at the Dramatic Workshop of the New York School of Social Research. There he studied Stanislavsky's acting techniques, before going to the Actor's Studio to work with Lee Strasberg and Stella Adler. Brando applied his 'method' training to summer stock roles, scoring enough rave reviews to merit his first shot at Broadway in 'I Remember Mama' (1944). Several acclaimed theatrical performances followed, including his landmark interpretation of the loutish Stanley Kowalski in Tennessee Williams' 'A Streetcar Named Desire' (1947), a role he was to brilliantly repeat on film in 1951. His first Oscar nomination was for Elia Kazan's powerfully disturbing 'On The Waterfront' (1954), a complex portrayal of Terry Malloy, the washed-up boxer turned mobster stooge. The following decade, Brando's career hit the doldrums. Undaunted, he concentrated his efforts towards ending racial discrimination and social injustice, becoming involved in the Civil Rights Movement. In 1972, he returned to movies, giving fans a lasting taste of his extraordinary acting genius, with his unforgettable portrayal of Don Vito Corleone in 'The Godfather'. Brando amplified his renewed notoriety by sending a little known actress, Maria Cruz, dressed in traditional Indian costume and calling herself Sacheen Littlefeather, to refuse the Best Actor Oscar on his behalf. This stemmed from his outrage over the plight of Native America. His appearances since then, with the exception of 'Last Tango in Paris' (1972), have mostly been highly paid cameos. He was again Oscar-nominated in 1989 for 'A Dry White Season', in which he parodied the role of Don Corleone. In 1994, he published his autobiography 'Songs My Mother Told Me'. Two of his three wives were the actresses Anna Kashfi and the Mexican star, Movita Castaneda.

Top Three Films:
'A Streetcar Named Desire' (1951)
'On The Waterfront' (1954)
'The Godfather' (1972)

'IT'S MINE' QUIPS BOB HOPE AS HE AND MARLON BRANDO FIGHT OVER BRANDO'S 1955 OSCAR FOR 'ON THE WATERFRONT' (1954)

THE GODDESSES

MARILYN MONROE

The personification of Hollywood glamour, shrouded by an unparalleled golden glow and rarefied charisma - few people could resist Marilyn. She was a voluptuous blonde, stealing the hearts of a nation and then the entire world with her astounding vital statistics (37-23-36) - pure iconic 50s Sex Goddess material. Born Norma Jean Mortenson on June 1 1926 in Los Angeles, her mother suffered from psychological problems and was eventually committed to a mental home. Young Norma spent much of her childhood in foster homes before marrying her childhood sweetheart Jimmy Dougherty, aged sweet sixteen. When Jimmy left for the South Pacific in 1944, Norma took a job on an assembly line. It was there that photographer David Conover spotted her and she made the cover of Yank magazine. Other modelling jobs followed, but on Jimmy's return she was forced to choose between career and marriage. In 1946, divorce papers split the pair for good and Marilyn put pen to paper contractually for 20th Century Fox instead. After what constituted tiny 'bit' parts, the former Norma Jean plumped for a change of image. She dyed her hair platinum blonde, became Marilyn Monroe and went on to make her debut in 'The Shocking Miss Pilgrim' (1947). It wasn't until 'The Asphalt Jungle' (1950), that cinema audiences were given the chance to watch her really shine. By 1953 her appeal had become universal and more has been written about Monroe than any other woman in show business. Her fame even superseded three broken marriages, though a fragility of character and self-destructive streak caused endless conflict with co-stars and directors. Still her career flourished and in 1956 she started her own motion picture company, producing hits like 'Bus Stop' (1956). 1960 saw her receiving a Golden Globe award for Best Actress in a Comedy for 'Some Like It Hot' (1959). On August 5, 1962, Monroe was found dead at her Brentwood home from a suspected drug overdose. There had been much speculation about the various highs and lows of her life, including her relationship with the unstoppable womaniser, John F. Kennedy. The breathy rendition of 'Happy Birthday Mr President', her gorgeous body swathed in a spray-on evening gown, has become the stuff of legends. For years to come, Marilyn Monroe will still be mourned as being the greatest sex symbol of all time.

Top Three Films:

'Gentlemen Prefer Blondes' (1953)
'Some Like it Hot' (1959)
'The Misfits' (1961)

MARILYN MONROE POSING BESIDE FRANK WORTH'S CAR

ELIZABETH TAYLOR

A strikingly beautiful child, Elizabeth Taylor was signed to a long-term contract by MGM and remained with the studio for almost twenty years. Today her name is synonymous with style and glamour. Married eight times, she is clearly a survivor and has taken on the role of the 'grand dame' of the American cinema. She played the lead in 'National Velvet' (1944). A few years on and Elizabeth had become very aware of her sexuality. In spite of great beauty, her talent as an actress was never fully realised although she excelled as Maggie the Cat in 'Cat on a Hot Tin Roof'. Her Oscar for 'Butterfield 8' was reported by some to be a sympathy award - she was seriously ill at the time and the industry had taken pity on her. Her personal life was as colourful as her career, marrying eight times, twice to actor Richard Burton. Taylor and Burton were one of the most glamorous film couples for nearly two decades and it was said that their acting in 'Cleopatra' reflected the intense feelings they had for one another at the beginning of their relationship. In the same way, their brilliant portrayal of an unhappily married couple in 'Who's Afraid of Virginia Woolf' (1966) mirrored the much publicised tempestuous relationship. In the 1980s, Elizabeth Taylor became active in AIDS awarness, after the tragic death of her friend Rock Hudson. In 1986 she launched a successful line of perfumes entitled 'Passion'. She was created a Dame of the British Empire in 2001.

Top Three Films:
'National Velvet' (1944)
'Cat on a Hot Tin Roof' (1958)
'Who's Afraid of Virginia Woolf?' (1966)

ELIZABETH TAYLOR APPEARS RATHER SERIOUS ON THE SET OF 'GIANT' (1956)

MARILYN MONROE

'Being a failure in Hollywood is like starving to death outside a banquet hall with the smells of filet mignon driving you crazy.'

Marilyn Monroe
(1955)

MARILYN MONROE IS HELPED WITH HER FUR STOLE BY HERBERT HOVER, OWNER OF CIRO'S

DAN DAILEY

The actor Dan Dailey, described by Betty Grable as *'The man with the mischievous grin and delicious blue eyes'*, graduated to the front of the chorus at the Roxy Theatre, New York during the early 1930s. This, in turn, led a part in the original 'Babes in Arms' (1937). Here he was spotted by MGM and signed to a year's contract. Despite his obvious song-and-dance abilities, the studio placed him in straight roles. When the contract expired, Dailey moved to 20th Century Fox and starred opposite Betty Grable in 'Mother Wore Tights' (1947). The duo soon became an immensely popular musical-comedy team with such winners as 'When My Baby Smiles at Me' (1948). As he grew older, his roles on screen dwindled. In 1975 tragedy struck when his only child, Dan Dailey III committed suicide. His devastated father died just three years later in October 1978.

Top Three Films:
'Lady Be Good' (1941)
'When My Baby Smiles at Me' (1948)
'There's No Business Like Show Business' (1955)

JANE RUSSELL

The generous cleavage of this voluptuous star provided the most crucial and controversial issue in the public showing of Howard Hughes's 'The Outlaw' (1943). Hughes, who produced the film (and originally found Russell working as a receptionist for his dentist), had even designed a brassiere to best advertise her assets. Billed as 'Mean, Moody and Magnificent', the world was invited to gaze in wonder. American censors almost immediately banned the film. Having survived this rather vulgar indignity, Russell subsequently displayed her less obvious talents, proficiently playing an assortment of roles - typically as a cynical, experienced dame. She adeptly portrayed exotic vixens and slightly shady, good-hearted ladies with aplomb. Russell survived the rigours of tinsel town because as she put it, *'I never took it or the promises that seriously'*. By the mid-70s she was appearing in TV commercials, advertising bras for Playtex. Today she resides in Malibu, California.

Top Three Films:
'The Outlaw' (1943)
'Macao' (1952)
'Gentlemen Prefer Blondes' (1953)

DAN DAILEY ADMIRES JANE RUSSELL'S DIAMONDS

BETTY GRABLE

Betty Grable appeared in several films in the 1930s and 40s, including 'Tin Pan Alley' (1940) and 'Pin Up Girl' (1944). A photograph of Grable wearing a bathing suit and looking over her shoulder, was widely held to be the most popular poster image for American soldiers in WWII. A prime pin-up with prime pins, Lloyd's of London even insured her legs for over one million dollars. Her career began at the tender age of three, when Grable's mother enrolled her at the Clark's Dancing School. Ten years later, and the pair were Hollywood bound, desperate for movie stardom. Grable firstly landed minor roles and then in 1932, signed a contract with RKO. It wasn't until almost a decade later when cinemagoers watched her in comedies such as 'Coney Island' and 'Sweet Rosie Grady' (both 1943) that they really began to sit up and take notice. In fact, Betty Grable became Hollywood's highest paid star of her time. By the mid 1950s, her screen career made way for Broadway shows. Both husbands, Jackie Coogan and Harry James, were in show business. A life long smoker, Grable lost her life to lung cancer and died in July 1973.

Top Three Films:
'Coney Island' (1943)
'Pin-Up Girl' (1944)
'How to Marry a Millionaire' (1953)

LAUREN BACALL, BETTY GRABLE AND MARILYN MONROE TAKE
A BREAK WHILST FILMING 'HOW TO MARRY A MILLIONAIRE' (1953)

ANN MILLER

A raven-tressed dancer whose style was likened to a blasting tornado, the gorgeous Ann Miller flashed her shapely legs in a number of Hollywood musicals during the 1940s and 50s. A professional dancer from childhood, Miller won a seven-year contract with RKO at the tender age of thirteen (claiming she was eighteen). She entered the movies as a bit-player in 1934, making her film debut in 'Anne of Green Gables'. In 1937, aged fourteen, she played Ginger Rogers' dancing partner in 'Stage Door', starting a film career spanning six decades. When Miller reached MGM, home of the most lavish movie musicals, she was too old, too tall and too brassy to play young ingenues, so was given secondary leads - some of them manipulative, temperamental dames. She danced with Fred Astaire in 'Easter Parade' (1948) and Gene Kelly in 'On the Town (1949). In 1953, she played Bianca in what is considered her finest film, 'Kiss Me Kate'. During the 1960s, she returned to the stage, travelling to Europe where she sang and danced 'Too Darn Hot' to the delight of five thousand soldiers in a 120 degrees heat. On to the 1980s, and Ann enjoyed tremendous success on Broadway with 'Sugar Babies', tapping those pins alongside the diminutive Mickey Rooney. Her recent screen comeback as the bejewelled Coco in David Lynch's 'Mulholland Drive' (2002) created a new generation of fans.

Top Three Films:
'Easter Parade' (1948)
'On the Town' (1952)
'Kiss Me Kate' (1953)

ARLENE DAHL

In recent years, Arlene Dahl has become most familiar to readership of The National Enquirer as their resident astrologer. Early on, her own stars bode good fortune with a succession of modelling and dancing jobs in her teens. Her foxy locks and piercing blue eyes were ideally suited to Technicolor and for a decade, she enjoyed steady success in undemanding roles. Dahl was over-indulged by the Studios. At MGM the famous designer Irene made her trousseau for her first marriage to Lex Barker. *"They knew our favourite clothes, our favourite colours, our favourite styles. I don't think anyone in the world was as spoiled as we were"*. She was considered one of New York society's richest women during the mid-seventies and later established herself as a businesswoman with Arlene Dahl Enterprises - marketing lingerie and cosmetics. Dahl's second husband was the actor Fernando Lamas and their son Lorenzo is also an actor. She currently resides in Beverly Hills.

Top Three Films:
'The Bride Goes West' (1948)
'Three Little Words' (1950)
'Jamaica Run' (1953)

MGM STARS: ELIZABETH TAYLOR, ANN MILLER (C) AND ARLENE DAHL (R)

GRACE KELLY

Alfred Hitchcock was completely smitten by what he referred to as Grace Kelly's *"sexual elegance"*, casting her in three of his most successful films: 'Dial M For Murder' (1954), 'Rear Widow' (1954) and 'To Catch a Thief' (1955). The golden beauty, destined to be real-life Princess, was born into old Philadelphia money in 1929. She adored the movies and even as a child, had just one goal; 'to become a star'. She trained at the American Academy of Dramatic Art and worked as a fashion model and in television commercials before graduating to stage parts. Not content with the work in New York, she moved to Southern California to pursue a career in motion pictures. MGM signed the twenty-two year old for a small part in 'Fourteen Hours' (1951). The next year, she co-starred in the part of Amy Kane, with Gary Cooper and Katy Jurado in 'High Noon' (1952). Then it was off to Africa for 'Mogambo' (1953), beating the bush with Ava Gardner and Clark Gable, and earning her a Best Supporting Actress nomination. Kelly's most outstanding work was under the direction of Hitchcock, and yet it was as the plain, long suffering wife of alcoholic Bing Crosby in 'The Country Girl' (1954) that she won her Best Actress Oscar. In 1956, Grace played the brittle and sexy Tracy Lord in 'High Society'. It turned out to be her final performance. While making 'To Catch a Thief' (1955), the Hollywood beauty had been introduced to an instantly smitten Prince Rainier of Monaco. Any sacrifices she might have made in swapping Hollywood for royalty, ultimately guaranteed that her star would never fade. This gorgeous lady enchanted the principality of Monaco right until her premature death in an car accident in 1982, just short of her 53rd birthday. She left behind Prince Rainier, three children and a legacy that will live forever.

Top Three Films:
'Rear Widow' (1954)
'To Catch a Thief' (1955)
'High Society' (1956)

GRACE KELLY AT THE PREMIERE OF 'REAR WINDOW' (1954)

AVA GARDNER

There was no doubting Gardner's extraordinary appeal when her photographs landed on the desk of notorious movie mogul, Louis B. Mayer, in 1941. (He reportedly cried, *'Find this girl, she's mine!'*). One year later, MGM signed her and subjected the nineteen-year-old to a gruelling schedule of speech therapy and acting training. She had over twenty small 'bit' parts, including 'Sunday Punch' (1942) and 'Maisie Goes to Reno' (1944), with Ann Sothern and newcomer Noreen Nash. It was not until 1946 that Gardner found herself playing the lead in the movie 'The Killers' (1946), a film noir crime drama, written by Ernest Hemingway and starring Burt Lancaster. The tag line read *'TENSE! TAUT! TERRIFIC! Told the untamed Hemingway way!'* Although her dramatic range was still rather narrow, she oozed glamour and her appeal meant that both sexes adored her. Perhaps as a result, she never believed in her own acting ability, but her latent talent was encouraged to the fore when coaxed out by superior directors, like John Ford in 'Mogambo' (1953) and George Cukor in 'Bhowani Junction' (1956). After three failed marriages (one to Frank Sinatra), dissatisfaction with the Hollywood merry-go-round prompted Ava to move to Spain in 1955, meaning that the majority of her subsequent films were made abroad. Stardom had made the country girl cosmopolitan, but she never overcame a deep insecurity about both her acting, and life in the spotlight. 'Night of the Iguana' (1964), seems, in her opinion, to have been her last quality piece of work, with later efforts completed strictly *"for the loot"*. In 1968, tax problems in Spain prompted a shift over to London, where Ava spent her last 22 years in reasonable comfort. Her film career wasn't instrumental in bringing any great personal fulfilment, but her looks may have detrimentally dictated the inevitable. Many fans still consider her the most beautiful actress in Hollywood history. Gardner died of pneumonia in London, in January 1990.

Top Three Films:
'Show Boat' (1951)
'On the Beach' (1960)
'The Night of the Iguana' (1964)

THE GLORIOUS AVA GARDNER (L) AND LANA TURNER

LANA TURNER

In search of greater job opportunities, Lana Turner and her mother moved to California. One school day shortly after their arrival, fifteen-year-old Turner went for a Cola at The Top Hat Café, a shop across the street from Hollywood High. In true legendary fashion, W.R. Wilkerson - publisher of the Hollywood Reporter - happened to be quenching his thirst at the same time. An introduction was made, a business card presented and the suggestion given that she call talent agent, Zeppo Marx. This, along with a letter Wilkerson personally wrote, helped team her with director Mervyn Le Roy. He put Turner on screen, changing her name from Julia Jean to Lana Turner. It was easy for her to relate to the role of schoolgirl Mary Clay in 'They Won't Forget' (1937) and though the part was relatively small, when the film was released she'd made her impact. Lana found herself tagged as 'The Sweater Girl,' thanks to a figure-hugging blue wool jumper that her character wore. She would win the hearts of every man in America, playing Cora Smith in 'The Postman Always Rings Twice' (1946), classic film noir that thrilled fans of doomed romance and double crosses. In 1948, Turner filmed 'The Three Musketeers' (her first Technicolor picture), her star then continuing to rise with Kirk Douglas in 'The Bad and The Beautiful' (1952). The film garnered an impressive five Academy Awards. It was also during this time that she started dating the dangerous mob associate, Johnny Stompanato. Turner fought to end the relationship but Stompanato was dangerously abusive, vowing she could never leave him and stay alive. During one such violent argument, her daughter Cheryl butted in, fearful that Stompanato would kill her mother. In her efforts to protect Turner, she attacked and fatally stabbed the mobster with a kitchen knife. The death was ruled as justifiable homicide and Cheryl was not incarcerated. Despite an Oscar nomination for 'Peyton Place' (1957), the regrettable scandal crippled Lana's career and she only briefly returned to the theatre. The challenges became even greater when her zest for life was dampened by the discovery of throat cancer. Turner rallied briefly, even accepting invitations to parties and opening nights. On June 29 1995, she died, Cheryl at her side.

Top Three Films:

'The Postman Always Rings Twice' (1946)
'The Merry Widow' (1952)
'The Bad and the Beautiful' (1952)

'Parties are not like they used to be. Let's face it, we all remember what Hollywood was like when stars were really stars, and glamour was truly glamour. I can remember planning what I was going to wear weeks before it happened. Clark Gable and Carole Lombard, Norma Shearer and Irving Thalberg, Joan Crawford, Myrna Loy and Loretta Young would be there to light up an exciting evening. It's so different now. Large groups of dissociated people seem to show up in anything from denims to loose robes – even the males'.

Lana Turner
(1976)

THE ESTABLISHMENT

ALAN LADD

Pint-sized American actor Alan Ladd literally entered motion pictures from the shadows, emerging as a fledgling reporter at the end of 'Citizen Kane' (1940). His mother emigrated from England, aged nineteen. His accountant father died when he was four. Aged five, Ladd set fire to their apartment whilst playing with matches. He was malnourished, undersized and nicknamed 'Tiny'. His mother then re-married, this time to a house painter who moved them to California when Ladd was just eight years old. He picked fruit, delivered papers, swept stores. In high school he discovered track and swimming. By 1931, Ladd was training for the 1932 Olympics, but an injury put pay to his efforts. Consequently he opened a hamburger stand, 'Tiny's Patio', then worked as a grip at Warner Bros. In 1936, he married Midge Jane Harold, but virtually penniless and to save on the rent, they decided to live apart - she with her mother. A year later, the couple moved into a friend's apartment and had their son, Alan Jr. Later that year, Ladd's mother moved in with them - a divorcee, destitute and alcoholic. Witnessing her agonising suicide from ant poison left Ladd totally traumatised. Talent scout Sue Carol discovered Ladd in 1939, whilst performing on radio. Carol had been a chorus cutie in Busby Berkeley musicals and, although her career had hit rock bottom, she was desperate to make Ladd a star. After finding him various 'bit' parts, he tested for 'This Gun for Hire' late in 1941. His fourth billing role as the psychotic killer Raven, gave him stardom and along with 'The Glass Key', brought Ladd a regular screen girlfriend in Veronica Lake. Throughout the 1940s, his tough-guy roles filled theatres and he was one of the few males whose cover photos sold movie magazines. In the 1950s, lucrative but unrewarding parts came his way - 'Shane' (1953) being the exception. By the end of the decade, alcohol and a string of poor movies had taken their poisonous toll. In November 1962, he was discovered unconscious and lying in a pool of blood with a bullet wound near his heart. Two years after that, apparently due to an accidental combination of alcohol and sedatives, Alan Ladd died.

Top Three Films:
'This Gun For Hire' (1942)
'The Blue Dahlia' (1946)
'Shane' (1953)

ALTHOUGH ALAN LADD AND HUMPHREY BOGART NEVER WORKED TOGETHER, FRANK WORTH MANAGED TO CAPTURE THE PAIR ON THE WARNER BROS. LOT

HUMPHREY BOGART

Humphrey Bogart is that extraordinary film phenomenon, a star whose personality, fame and following are much greater today than they were during his lifetime. Although he held considerable appeal for the three decades from the mid-1930s, there was never any suggestion that he would be nominated to heart throb status. Since his death in 1957 and the subsequent cult that has grown up around such films as 'Casablanca' (1943) and 'The Big Sleep' (1946), Bogart has become one of the most potent male symbols ever to grace the screen. The son of a Manhattan surgeon and a magazine illustrator, he wasn't a dedicated student and on expulsion from Phillips Military Academy, joined the US Navy. On return to civilian life he befriended family neighbour William Brady, a leading theatre impresario, and entered the world of show business. Shortly after the end of WWI, Bogart began to appear on stage and by 1930, won a contract with Fox Studios. His debut in 'Broadway's Like That' (1930), a ten-minute Joan Blondell short, was followed by five years of stage and minor film roles, including the John Ford comedy 'Up the River' (1930) with Broadway émigré Spencer Tracy and 'Love Affair' (1931) with Dorothy Mackail. *"Bogie was mean, menacing and marvellous,"* recalled Mackail in 1988. *"Warner Brothers gave him some opportunities to flex his stuff and gave him the freedom to construct his own style that continued long after I was completely forgotten"*. His appearance as the wild-eyed drunk, Duke Mantee, in Robert Sherwood's play 'The Petrified Forest' and the subsequent cinematic version, changed public opinion. Most of his earlier films were not great classics but his presence made them unforgettable. Bogart seemed to thrive on tempestuous relationships, constantly arguing with Jack Warner at the studios, who eventually acknowledged Bogey's growing popularity in gangster roles. The star later thanked George Raft for allowing him to shine in the two films that he'd initially turned down - as Sam Spade in 'The Maltese Falcon' (1940) and as Roy 'Mad Dog' Earle, in 'High Sierra' (1941). Two years later he was nominated for an Oscar as the unforgettable Rick in 'Casablanca'. Through the 1950s, Bogart made a dozen films, unquestionably the greatest being 'The African Queen' (1955) with the marvellous Katharine Hepburn. Away from the public gaze, he was a sailing fanatic who totally adored his fourth wife, Lauren Bacall, to his dying day. Cancer claimed the rugged star's life on January 14 1957.

Top Three Films:

'The Maltese Falcon' (1941)
'The Big Sleep' (1946)
'The African Queen' (1955)

Beverly Roberts was definitely a star, and clearly fitted the pattern of Warner Bros. leading ladies of the 1930s who were young, beautiful, blunt and fearless. She worked with Errol Flynn, Humphrey Bogart and Pat O'Brien.

'Bogey was marvellous, interesting, and complex. He had a wonderful ego. But, with Bogey, that ego was directed towards the achievement of something good for the picture he was working on. He was not star-centred. He was an achievement-centred person. And, as a result, he could be difficult as far as the studio was concerned. He and I got along famously because he respected me as an actor. We were members of the original Rat Pack. But there was no funny business (sex), just good times and great intelligent conversation'.

Beverly Roberts
(2002)

FRED ASTAIRE

No dancer in the entire history of the silver screen won greater frame than Fred Astaire. Yet all through his career he was the most casual and disarming of all the Hollywood's Greats. His was a simmering ambition that never aimed to ignite a career by fireworks. He shrugged off setbacks and stalemates with the same charming detachment with which he also accepted greater triumphs. Astaire never thought he would succeed in Hollywood, but was pushed to try his luck after his sister Adele quit their Broadway act to marry Lord Cavendish in 1932. RKO recognised the potential and cast him with Ginger Rogers in 'Flying Down to Rio' (1933). The male lead in the picture, Gene Raymond, recalled *"I was driving along Hollywood Boulevard days after the opening, only to see tens of thousands cheering Astaire and Rogers' amazing 'Carioca' dance sequence. When he came back to Hollywood he was enthusiastically welcomed as a movie star"*. With Ginger Rogers by his professional side, the next sixteen years meant that his prodigious reputation as the world's supreme song-and-dance man, was irrefutably made. After the demise of their partnership, Astaire continued to dance with a variety of actresses including Cyd Charisse, Judy Garland and Leslie Caron. During the 60s, he tried out in straight roles, in 1974 receiving an Oscar nomination for his performance in 'The Towering Inferno' (1974), where fans lapped-up his old musical magic, dancing with Jennifer Jones. Afterwards, he put his tap shoes away, feeling he could no longer attain the high standards he'd once reached. But he could and did continue in character roles, the last being in 'Ghost Story' (1981). Later that year, the American Film Institute bestowed on him their prestigious Life Achievement Award. In 1987, the much loved Fred Astaire danced his way to the heavens, and was buried at Oakwood Memorial Park, Chatsworth, in California - also the final resting place of Ginger Rogers, some eight years later.

Top Three Films:
'The Gay Divorcee' (1934)
'Top Hat' (1935)
'Silk Stockings' (1957)

FRED ASTAIRE RELAXES AT A LOS ANGELES SPORTS EVENT

CLARK GABLE

Clark Gable epitomised the dichotomy of movie madness. Crowned the 'King of Hollywood' early on in his career, he'd also been less favourably likened to 'an ugly Toby jug'. Lionel Barrymore, who had cast Gable in his Broadway production 'The Cooperhead', initially fought to persuade MGM studio boss, Irving Thalberg, to hire his friend. Gable's enormous ears horrified Thalberg, whilst actress Muriel Evans attested to *"dreadful halitosis"*. Jack Warner also turned the actor away. Gable was about to call it a day when Thalberg called him back to the Culver City lot. After consideration (and some gentle persuasion from his wife Norma Shearer), he placed Gable opposite Anita Page in 'The Easiest Way' (1931). *"He was a doll,"* exclaimed Anita in August 2002. *"He could be fresh though and often made a pass. I was a huge star and had no interest in Clark Gable"*. Years later when he worked with Grace Kelly, Gable compared her charm and beauty to Anita Page's. The film that took Gable to the top was 'A Free Soul' (1931). Fans loved his manhandling of Norma Shearer. This apart, his unshaven lovemaking with a braless Jean Harlow in 'Red Dust' (1932) completely sent the already adoring fans over the edge. Clark Gable was the idol of millions, the recipient of 40,000 fan letters a month. By the end of the decade and bathing in the success of 'It Happened One Night' (1934) and 'San Francisco' (1936), he grabbed his true crown, 'King of Hollywood'. Bette Davis was the 'Queen'. Gable's greatest triumph has to be as Rhett Butler in 'Gone With the Wind' (1939). Infact the author of the book, Margaret Mitchell, later claimed that Rhett was actually based on the charismatic star. For a further twenty years he acted in one success after another. His last role, opposite Marilyn Monroe in John Huston's classic 'The Misfits' (1961), was a final tribute to a superb actor. The third of his five wives was Carole Lombard. Gable died in 1960.

Top Three Films:
'It Happened One Night' (1934)
'Gone With the Wind' (1939)
'The Misfits' (1961)

CLARK GABLE AND HIS WIFE, KAY SPRECKLES-GABLE, ATTEND THE 27TH ANNUAL ACADEMY AWARDS

JOAN CRAWFORD

The early life of Joan Crawford, formally Lucille Fay LeSueur, reads like one of the silent melodramas she'd watched on-screen as a child. Jon Denson, President of her fan club, said *'When Joan had to cry for a scene, all she had to do was think of her tragic early life, and the tears would fall'*. History repeated itself when Crawford's own adopted children - in particular, Christina - fell victim to her wrath. Christina posthumously attacked her mother's alleged cruelty, in the best-selling book 'Mommie Dearest'. Faye Dunaway then depicted her as a bitch goddess in the 1981 movie version. At the picture's release, alarmed contemporaries like Gloria Swanson barked: *'No daughter should tear apart their mother like that'*. But Crawford was unlike any other movie star. She oozed glamour and possessed a screen presence that left audiences reeling in awe. Joan started out as a dancer and model, eventually acting in some early and rather risqué silent movie shorts. After a stint in nightclubs, she was given the chance to join the chorus of 'Innocent Eyes' (1924) on Broadway. Spotted by a talent scout she signed an MGM contract. Crawford clawed her way to stardom, eventually becoming the third most popular actress under studio control. Crawford transformed herself throughout the decades, from jazz baby to stylish fashion icon. By the 30s, she was coming into her own and headlining entire pictures. In the 40s, she became the strong-willed, intelligent woman destroying all and sundry in her way. Dropped by MGM in 1944, Crawford was snapped up by Warner Bros, where her career was given an enormous boost in the guise of the tortured mother in 'Mildred Pierce' - an Oscar winning performance. A decade on, Crawford found herself submerged by a new breed of actor, yet she remained determined to bask in the limelight, the epitome of the hard and fast movie star. Her worst nightmare was to lose the fame, even if it meant taking roles that were way below her. Joan Crawford died on the morning of May 10 1977, just as her maid was delivering a batch of fan letters to her. A tender and poignantly fitting goodbye.

Top Three Films:
'Grand Hotel' (1932)
'Mildred Pierce' (1945)
'Whatever Happened to Baby Jane?' (1962)

JOAN CRAWFORD, FRESH FROM COMPLETING 'SUDDEN FEAR' (1953), POSES WITH GLENN FORD

GLENN FORD

His father was a Canadian railroad executive, moving the family from Quebec to Santa Monica in 1924. At this time, Glenn Ford - a budding actor by the age of eight – showed a blatant talent that flourished both at high school and in leading roles for small theatre groups. In 1939 he landed a screen test for Columbia Studios and a subsequent contract. He was loaned out to 20th Century Fox for his first movie 'Heaven with a Barbed Wire Fence' (1939). Over the next forty-five years Ford notched up almost one hundred movies - often as the leading man. His career was interrupted only once to join the Marines during WWII. During military service in France, Ford helped build safe houses for those hiding from the Nazis. He is most fondly remembered for playing opposite the ravishing Rita Hayworth in 'Gilda' (1946), as well as a string of great Westerns including '3:10 to Yuma' (1957). Glenn Ford's first wife was the tap dancing sensation Eleanor Powell.

Top Three Films:
'Gilda' (1946)
'The Big Heat' (1953)
'3:10 to Yuma' (1957)

Actress Arline Judge said of the diminutive Mildred Shay, star of 'The Women' and Balalaika' (both 1939): *'Mildred is the only actress to come to Hollywood a virgin and leave in the same condition!'* Mildred knew everyone in tinsel town, including Frank Worth and Joan Crawford.

'My first real part was as Helene, the French maid to Crystal Allen (Joan Crawford) in 'The Women'. I can recall this funny looking guy snapping away whenever George Cukor wasn't around. Worth was a nice guy; he just looked as if his mother had dressed him. As for Joan Crawford, well, I respected her she was very sweet to me. We once sat in her trailer, knitting'.

Mildred Shay
(2002)

GARY COOPER

Gary Cooper began his career as an extra in Hollywood, earning just ten dollars per day. A conservative guess puts him in around fifty movies during his first two years, including many Tom Mix westerns. Paramount snapped up the tall, handsome, softly spoken twenty-seven year old for the small role of a reporter in 'Wings' (1927) with Clara Bow. She was smitten and asked for Cooper on her next picture 'Children of Divorce' (1927) - his first excursion into romantic movies. Off screen, Cooper was also proving to be a fabulous lover to the likes of Bow, Evelyn Brent, Fay Wray, Lupe Velez and Judith Allen. A big hit in the saddle, few could match his excellence as a star on the Western plains. He made the transition from silent film to 'talkies' with ease, earning an Oscar nomination for 'Mr Deeds Goes to Town' (1936) and then winning the Academy Award for Best Actor for 'Sergeant York' (1941). By the end of WWII, Cooper's career had hit the doldrums. Then in 1952, Fred Zinnemann cast him as the embattled Marshal Will Kane, abandoned by the townspeople in 'High Noon' (1952). A second Oscar rewarded his powerful talent and moreover led to better parts once again. Gary Cooper made his very last film, 'The Naked Age' in 1961, and died that same year in Beverly Hills, California.

Top Three Films:
'Morocco' (1930)
'Mr. Deeds Goes to Town' (1936)
'High Noon' (1952)

FRANCES DEE

Frances Dee ventured into motion pictures with the arrival of sound, urging producers at Fox to hire her because of 'great theatrical experience'. The break came when Maurice Chevalier picked her as his leading lady in 'Playboy in Paris' (1930). Three years later, Dee met actor Joel McCrea whilst filming 'The Silver Cord'. Following a whirlwind romance, the two were married. Dee continued to act mostly in ingénue roles throughout the 30s, notably as Margaret in 'Little Women' (1933). Her film career faded during the mid-forties and in 1945 she embarked on a stage career, before taking her final curtain call in 1953. The nonagenarian actress recently made a huge splash appearing alongside 1930s actress Marion Shilling at the 1998 Memphis Film Festival in Tunica, Mississippi.

Top Three Films:
'Little Women' (1933)
'King of the Jungle' (1933)
'Becky Sharp' (1935)

GARY COOPER AND FRANCES DEE IN INTENSE DISCUSSION WITH COOPER'S WIFE, SANDRA SHAW

JOHN WAYNE

With the unlikely name of Marion Morrison, the tall, lean giant of the silver screen became known as John Wayne, the biggest box office star in movie history. Wayne, or "Duke" (a name poached from the family dog), was a keen football player, narrowly missing a position at Annapolis University but instead moving to the University of California. Cowboy star, Tom Mix, was the first to introduce Wayne to the movies, helping him obtain work as a prop man. Good-looking and prominent, he was quickly snapped-up by directors to play 'bit' parts in silent movies - 'Bardleys the Magnificent' (1926), being his first with Eleanor Boardman. After more than seventy-five low-budget adventures, John Ford cast him as The Ringo Kid in 'Stagecoach' (1939). Overnight, a great star was born. When Emperor Hirohito of Japan visited America, with an open opportunity to meet the masses, his ultimate request was for none other than John Wayne. Two Oscar nominations came Wayne's way. The first being for 'The Sands of Iwo Jima' (1949), but he eventually got to hold the Oscar statuette in his hands for 'True Grit' (1969). The statuesque star endured many onscreen romances, but his partnership with Maureen O'Hara lingered most fondly, working harmoniously together on 'Rio Grande' (1950) and 'The Quiet Man' (1953). Away from the screen, Wayne entertained thousands over the airways with his radio series 'The Three Sheets to the Wind' (1944). Attempts to break free of the saddle seemed ill advised. During the 1960s and 70s Wayne appeared in many screen classics once again, securing his name as a very bankable movie star. In 1976 he made his last film 'The Shootist' opposite the equally well-loved James Stewart. Wayne died in June 1979.

Top Three Films:
'Stagecoach' (1939)
'The Searchers' (1956)
'True Grit' (1969)

JOHN WAYNE JOKES WITH JAKE LA MOTTA, WORLD MIDDLEWEIGHT BOXING CHAMPION (1949-51)

MAE WEST

Hollywood's most unlikely sex symbol was an incredible forty years old by the time that her star rose. A veteran of burlesque, and standing a mere five feet tall, Mae seduced the male population with her cracking one-liners. Hers was a lethally attractive combination of an acid tongue, pouting lips, heavy eyes and slow sexy wiggle. (During WWII, army crewman in the Pacific named their inflatable life vests after Mae, terminology that's still used to this day). Actress and former Paramount starlet, Grace Bradley, described her gait to be *"Like a love struck hippopotamus"*. The infamous phrase *'Come up and see me some time'* pushed Mae into legendary status and went to helping Paramount studios - where she was under contract - avoid bankruptcy. Mae was born in 1982 to 'Battling Jack' West, a wrestler, and Matilda Doelger. Her father introduced his daughter to vaudeville when she was just five. Recalling those early days, Mae quipped, *"Some of those circuits that I worked were no place for a lady, but then I was no lady"*. She seldom went to school, instead preferring to perform on stage. By the time of her fourteenth birthday, her billing as 'Baby Vamp' showed her potential as a sure-fire hit. West had been writing plays since the 1920s, most notably the scandalous 'SEX', which resulted in her arrest. But this was just typical audacity and she triumphed again with 'Diamond Lil'. Her film career began in 1932 when she played little more than a 'bit' part in 'Night After Night' (1932). By all accounts she was unhappy with the role and re-wrote all her dialogue. Only in her first three films did she have full rein. The ensuing censorship clampdown weakened but failed to destroy her indomitable spirit. As the years took their toll, Mae had some minor surgery around her eyes, then opting for sticky tape to keep her face buoyant, which was further caked by lashings of foundation, powder and heavy rouge. Walter Pidgeon, who worked with Mae on her final film 'Sextette' (1978) said *"God help the wardrobe mistress who had to look after Mae when she took off her bra. Why, when they're set loose, the floor would most certainly go."* On West's death in 1980, rumors were flying around New York and Los Angeles that Mae had infact been a man. Edith Head, the multi-award winning costume designer said at the time: *"I've seen Mae West without a stitch on and she's all woman. No hermaphrodite could have those bosoms"*. Head then poetically described them as *"two very large melons"*. Breasts quite apart, Mae West was an indisputable original.

Top Three Films:
'Some Down Him Wrong' (1933)
'My Little Chickadee' (1940)
'Myra Breckinridge' (1970)

MAE WEST PROVES SHE IS STILL DIAMOND LIL'

JAMES CAGNEY

Cinema's quintessential 'tough guy', Cagney made his screen debut in 1930 and the following year, gave a startling performance as gangster Tom Powers (who shoves a grapefruit into Mae Clarke's face) in 'The Public Enemy' (1931), that launched him towards great stardom. James Cagney actually started life as a street kid from New York City, born into a working class family. A talented hoofer with an aptitude for light comedy, he effortlessly caught the attention of Hollywood talent scouts. Signed to Warner Bros, Cagney was placed in back-to-back star vehicles, tailor made for the tough guy image. The climax of his Warner's stint came with 'Yankee Doodle Dandy' (1942). His portrayal of pioneering Broadway showman George M. Cohen earned Cagney his one and only Academy Award. The star became the subject of many impersonators yet curiously, he never actually uttered the phrase *"You dirty rat"*, for which he was most famous. In 1981, Cagney ventured out from his farm on Martha's Vineyard to play a crusty police commissioner in 'Ragtime'. He died in Stanfordville, New York in March 1986.

Top Three Films:
'The Public Enemy' (1931)
'Angels with Dirty Faces' (1938)
'Yankee Doodle Dandy' (1942)

FRANK McHUGH

Frank McHugh was a popular Warner Bros. contract player of the 1930s, appearing in over ninety films between 1930-42. A close friend of Spencer Tracy, James Cagney and Pat O'Brien, McHugh was integrated into their fraternity, enjoying their friendship at the racetrack, football games and Hollywood hot spots. A punchy routine and nervous comedic laugh became his trademark. When Cagney returned to the screen in 'Ragtime' (1981), McHugh sent him a telegram which read, *"Walk, don't run! And make sure you avoid light coloured trousers; they show up dribbles, which at our wild ages is inevitable!"* He died in Greenwich, Connecticut, 1981.

Top Three Films:
'The Front Page' (1931)
'A Midsummer Night's Dream' (1935)
'State Fair' (1945)

FROM LEFT TO RIGHT: JAMES CAGNEY, FRANK MCHUGH, PAT O'BRIEN AND SPENCER TRACY

PAT O'BRIEN

No other leading man in Hollywood played as many cops, servicemen or priests as Pat O'Brien. He delivered his lines with an Irish accent that, although rather stereotypical, more than pleased his movie audiences. He could also, on occasions, play smooth-talking con men and kind-hearted lovers. As a boyhood friend of Spencer Tracy, they attended military school, joined the navy and went to Drama College together in New York. He was also a good dancer, making his mark on Broadway during the late 1920s. O'Brien landed roles during the earliest days of sound in movies like 'The Front Page' (1931) with Mary Brian, 'American Madness' (1932) with Constance Cummings and 'China Clipper' (1936) with Beverly Roberts. He and Roberts became the very best of friends and recently she recalled *"Pat and I were at Warner Brothers who, unlike the high gloss churned out by MGM, made more realistic films for the common man"*. O'Brien went on to star in well over one hundred movies in a career that spanned fifty years. He married aspiring actress Eloise Taylor in 1931, though the pair only appeared professionally once together in a stage version of 'On Golden Pond' in 1983. He died that same year.

Top Three Films:
'China Clipper' (1936)
'Angels with Dirty Faces' (1938)
'Fighting with Father Dunne' (1948)

SPENCER TRACY

Early theatrical ventures confirmed Spencer Tracy's desire to become an actor. He toured with a stock company in White Plains, New York, when in 1930, his break came in the guise of 'Killer' Mears in 'The Last Mile'. John Ford saw his potential and cast him in his first movie 'Up the River' (1930), made at Fox. From there Tracy moved to MGM, where he would remain for the next twenty years. Spencer entered the record books by winning the first ever back-to-back Best Actor Oscar, in both 1937 and 1938. Despite a career that heralded such memorable roles as Elizabeth Taylor's father in 'Father of the Bride' (1950), Tracy will always be best remembered for his enduring love affair and the nine movies he made with Katharine Hepburn. She was with Tracy in June 1967, on the day he suffered a fatal heart attack at their Beverly Hills home.

Top Three Films:
'Captain Courageous' (1937)
'Adam's Rib' (1949)
'Bad Day at Black Rock' (1955)

Addie McPhail played the ingénue in countless films from the earliest days of sound. She and Roscoe 'Fatty' Arbuckle married in 1932.

'Frank McHugh was the cleaner, odd job man, cop or priest, but never the lead. Everybody loved him in Hollywood, including my then husband Roscoe. Because of the nature of his roles, Frank worked with everyone at Warner Brothers. We appeared together in 'Corsair' (1931), an odd adventure film with Thelma Todd'.

Addie McPhail
(2002)

JAMES STEWART

James Maitland Stewart holds the eternal title of one of the best loved of the Hollywood Greats. *"I'd like people to remember me as someone who was good at his job"* he said. *"And someone who seemed to mean what he said"*. His querulous drawl and gangly appearance were endearing trademarks. Stewart was the first movie star to enter service for WWII, joining one year before the bombing of Pearl Harbour. He eventually became Colonel Stewart and was the most decorated movie star in the history of the war. Having graduated from Princeton University with an architecture degree, he then 'trod the boards' with Maureen O'Sullivan, Henry Fonda and the University Players. All three went on to perform on Broadway, before Hollywood beckoned in 1935. His early successes included an Oscar winning performance as the young, bashful idealist in Frank Capra's, 'Mr. Smith Goes to Washington' (1939), as the seemingly gun-shy sheriff in 'Destry Rides Again' (1939) and another Oscar winning role as the fast talking reporter under Katharine Hepburn's spell in 'The Philadelphia Story' (1940). After the war, Stewart returned to Hollywood, teaming up with Frank Capra for the hugely popular 'It's a Wonderful Life' (1947). Dropping the stammer, he forged on to play a crusading reporter in 'Call Northside 777' (1948), as well as the eccentric drunk conversing with a giant white rabbit in 'Harvey' (1950). This was followed by a series of Westerns including 'The Naked Spur' (1953). Alfred Hitchcock favoured him for 'Rear Window' (1954), 'The Man Who Knew Too Much' (1956) and 'Vertigo' (1958), roles that he played with much aplomb. Stewart's star continued to shine in 'Two Rode Together' (1961) and as the tenderfoot lawyer in 'The Man Who Shot Liberty Valance' (1962) with John Wayne. The two cinematic giants were again reunited for 'The Shootist' (1976). His last cinematic foray was 'An American Tail: Fievel Goes West' (1991) for which he supplied the voice of the aged sheriff, Wylie Burp. James Stewart's death in 1997 cemented the end of the Golden Age of Hollywood and the departure of a hugely loved and much respected hero of the people.

Top Three Films:
'It's a Wonderful Life' (1947)
'Rear Window' (1954)
'Vertigo' (1958)

FAMILY MAN JAMES STEWART, WITH HIS WIFE GLORIA AND STEPSONS, RONALD AND MICHAEL

ALFRED HITCHCOCK

As one of the British film industry's highest paid directors, the larger-than-life Alfred Hitchcock left for Hollywood in 1932, where all but three of his remaining films were made. In 1955, he became an American citizen and shortly before his death in 1980, was knighted. The son of an Essex shopkeeper, Hitchcock trained as an engineer, later turning to the study of art. While working as a fifteen-shilling-a-week clerk in an advertising agency, he tried to earn a living by writing titles for silent films. The 'Famous Players' studio - who were making films in Islington, North London at the time - gave him a job, thus embarking on a then unstoppable career. His wife, Alma Reville, was a scriptwriter who collaborated on many scenario projects. More has been written about Hitchcock than any other director, ranging from intricate Catholic theology to various symbolic interpretations of the appearances he perpetually made in his films. Hitchcock's greatest achievements came during the mid-to-late 50s with such classic thrillers as 'North By Northwest' (1959) and 'Psycho' (1960). Actress Joan Marion, who had a 'bit' part in 'Champagne' (1929) summed it up with: *'Hitchcock had an almost banal view of his work, loved his leading ladies to the point of obsession and had the most famous profile in cinematic history'.*

Top Three Films:
'Blackmail' (1929)
'Vertigo' (1958)
'Psycho' (1960)

ALFRED HITCHCOCK, GRACE KELLY AND OLEG CASSINI AT THE PREMIERE OF 'REAR WINDOW' (1954)

BETTE DAVIS

Bette Davis became known as one of the silver screen's greatest actresses of all time. She chain-smoked and flashed her saucer-like eyes through one hundred movies, earning herself an unbelievable ten Oscar nominations. When she started to complain about being given poor roles, Jack Warner tried to call her bluff by signing little known British actress, Joan Marion, to replace Davis at Warner Bros. But Bette was no push-over. The star endured these and other battles with the studio before she was able to prove herself worthy of better and higher paid parts in A-list pictures. Nobody had properly reckoned on her popular allure. Davis won her first Oscar for 'Dangerous' (1935) and her second for 'Jezebel' (1938). By 1940, she had become the biggest star in Hollywood, second only to Clark Gable. She was at the zenith of her career when suddenly and shockingly her popularity waned, though thankfully not for long. In 1950 she bounced back, brilliantly playing the faded Broadway star Margo Channing in 'All About Eve'. Later that decade, she faltered for a second time, fighting her way back as a demented former child star and tormenting her crippled sister (played by Joan Crawford) in 'Whatever Happened to Baby Jane' (1962). Despite some often dire scripts, Davis' determination and rigid work ethic kept her on track. Her personal life was less successful, marrying four times and suffering severe bouts of ill health - including two strokes. In 1985 her estranged daughter B.D. Hyman wrote 'My Mothers Keeper', an horrific account of her childhood tormented by Davis. It was met with the same public hysteria that greeted Christina Crawford on publication of 'Mommie Dearest', her damning account of life at the hands of Joan Crawford. Davis spent the last years of her life touring the globe, and collecting Lifetime Achievement Awards. Her last significant role was as Lillian Gish's elder sister, Libby in 'The Whales of August' (1987). She died returning from the 1989 San Sebastian Film Festival.

Top Three Films:
'Dark Victory' (1939)
'Now Voyager' (1942)
'What Ever Happened to Baby Jane?' (1962)

BETTE DAVIS STANDS ALONGSIDE OSCAR WINNERS, MARLON BRANDO AND GRACE KELLY, AT THE 27TH ANNUAL ACADEMY AWARDS

THE SEX KITTENS

JAYNE MANSFIELD

Hollywood or bust? Blonde and mesmerisingly voluptuous, Jayne Mansfield became a renowned sexpot of both Hollywood and Italian-produced movies of the 1950s and 60s. Married at sixteen to high school sweetheart, Paul Mansfield, and becoming a mother at 17, she started out as a physics major, switching first to drama at the University of Texas and then later to UCLA. After she and her husband had parted company, she joined a Dallas stock company and headed to Hollywood in 1954, on the advice of a boyfriend. Mansfield used her exceptional I.Q. (reportedly 163) to smartly break into movies via a series of incredible publicity stunts and thus became a household name, even before appearing in a film. After bleaching her hair, she won a few beauty contests and did some TV work before then making her screen debut in 'Pete Kelly's Blues' (1955) with Peggy Lee. Soon afterwards, her contract was dropped. Ironically, Mansfield's big break came by way of the Broadway stage, where she starred in the smash Broadway hit, 'Will Success Spoil Rock Hunter?' The success of the play landed her a seven-year contract with 20th Century-Fox and a starring role in 'The Girl Can't Help It' (1956). To her chagrin, Mansfield never seemed to gain the same recognition that was bestowed on Marilyn Monroe. But her career kept her busy and in addition to movies, she had a successful Vegas act, a brief singing and recording career, as well as a string of nightclub performances and television guest spots. Tragedy cut her life short. In the early hours of June 29 1967, Mansfield, accompanied by her boyfriend, Sam Brody and their 20-year-old driver, were all killed when their 1966 Buick Electra ploughed into the back of a large truck..

Top Three Films:

'The Girl Can't Help It' (1956)
'Will Success Spoil Rock Hunter?' (1957)
'A Guide for the Married Man' (1967)

A PLAYFUL JAYNE MANSFIELD POSES FOR FRANK WORTH

KIM NOVAK

She might have appeared the classical Hollywood sex goddess - blonde, buxom and owing her initial success to a sparkling physical allure - but Kim Novak (Columbia Studios' answer to Marilyn Monroe) developed into a capable and at times, first-rate actress. Novak, who at this stage was still going by her real name of Marilyn, was originally going to be re-christened Kit Marlowe. She wanted to at least keep her family name of Novak, so the young actress and studio personnel plumped for Kim. She had a number of 'bit' parts early on before wowing audiences in the hit movie 'Pal Joey' (1957) with Frank Sinatra and Rita Hayworth. Despite being crucified by the critics, the film did extremely well in the cinemas, though Kim was never over-enamoured of her role. She was also sensitive to the fact that Rita Hayworth got the lion's share of attention. In 1958, she appeared in a dual role of Judy Barton and Madeleine Elster in Alfred Hitchcock's classic 'Vertigo', with James Stewart. Popular opinion puts Novak's best role as Lillian Anderson Munnsen in the thriller, 'Liebestraum' (1991). Today, she's known as an passionate animal lover, keeping horses and llamas at her Eagle Point home in Oregan. And from time to time, is also spotted feeding another of her interests – checking out the latest fashions at the Designer shows.

Top Three Films:

'Pal Joey' (1957)
'Vertigo' (1958)
'Kiss Me, Stupid' (1964)

NAUGHTY GIRLS! DEBBIE REYNOLDS AND KIM NOVAK (L) ENJOY DESSERT TOGETHER

VAMPIRA

Vampira, star of Ed Wood's 'Plan 9 From Outer Space' (1958), was once the most famous ghoul on American television. Contracted as the hostess on Channel 7 KABC's late night horror movie, Vampira's presence easily out-shone the Z-grade movies that were showing. To say that her segment was dramatic is a miniscule understatement. After eerie organ music from Holst's 'The Planets, came a close-up of a spider's web in the middle of which her pet arachnid, Rollo, waited for his prey. Next, Vampira would emerge through a mist of dry ice, clawing the air with long scarlet talons, varnished a haemorrhage red. She'd scream, *'I am Vampira. I hope you all had the good fortune to have a terrible week!'* The unparalleled scene was utterly sensational, but parental groups blasted the network calling Vampira sadistic and demanding her removal. Born Maila Nurmi in Petsamo, Finland in 1919, she initially decided on an acting career, much against her parental wishes. Not that it stopped her. At the age of seventeen, Maila took a room just outside Hollywood. Between acting jobs she danced and modelled, and became friends with Marilyn Monroe and Irish McCalla. Whilst dancing at the Florentine Gardens, she was spotted by producer Hunt Stromberg, who put her under contract to Channel 7. After Vampira's television show ended, she worked in films - including the detective flick, 'The Beat Generation', 'Too Much Too Soon' (both 1959) with Errol Flynn, and 'Sex Kittens go to College' (1960). She spent the 60s touring her spooky act and by the 70s was reduced to selling grave rubbings of famous dead movie stars. Still in Gothic mode, the 80s saw her fronting the punk band, 'Vampira and Satan's Cheerleaders'. Today, her time is spent caring for stray animals (*"I have been befriending strays all my life"*), as well as successfully launching her own web site, 'Vampira's Attic' in 2001.

Top Three Films:

'Too Much Too Soon' (1958)
'Plan 9 From Outer Space' (1958)
'The Beat Generation' (1959)

HORROR HOSTESS, VAMPIRA

MAMIE VAN DOREN

Of Hollywood's three M's (Monroe, Mansfield and Mamie), only Mamie is still living, endorsing her claim that *"I survived because I didn't go down the same road as those girls: the road to destruction"*. Van Doren was described as "The poor man's Lana Turner", and is best remembered for a series of showy roles in cheap 1950s melodramas, emphasising her physical endowments rather than her dramatic abilities. A former dance-band singer, her first movie 'Jet Pilot' (1950) was considered to be on such shaky ground, that the release date was withheld until 1957. Throughout the next decade, she continued in flimsy drive-in quickies and sexploitation films. In 1987, Van Doren published her autobiography, 'Playing the Field'; a highly amusing account of her affairs with Hollywood stars including Warren Beatty, Steve Cochran, Steve McQueen and the singer Tom Jones. A truly 'open' spirit, Mamie recently commissioned her own web site. It shows an astonishingly good tour of her hedonistic life, including images of 'Mamie Today' - stripped to the waist and readily displaying her ample measurements (38-34-35). A frequent guest at Hugh Hefner's Playboy Mansion, she's recently returned to the fore appearing on the BBC's 'Hot Wax' show, with host Ruby Wax, and on the silver screen in 'Slackers' (2002).

Top Three Films:
'High School Confidential!' (1958)
'The Beat Generation' (1959)
'Sex Kittens Go to College' (1960)

RICHARD LONG

The rugged Hollywood actor of the 1950s and 60s arrived in Hollywood via a contract to Universal Studios. Although he made an impact on screen with roles opposite stars like, Claudette Colbert, Burt Lancaster and Rosemary de Camp, Long failed to reach the same height of stardom as his contemporaries. Television was where he found his niche, where he became best known for his roles in the western series "The Big Valley" and the comedy "Nanny and the Professor". Long succumbed to a long-standing heart ailment on December 21 1974. Both wives, Suzan Ball and Maria Corday were actresses, the latter survived him.

Top Three Films:
'Tomorrow is Forever' (1946)
'House on Haunted Hill' (1958)
'The Big Valley' (1965)

THE ULTIMATE SEX KITTEN, MAMIE VAN DOREN TINKERS WITH HER CAR (AIDED BY RICHARD LONG)

ROSEMARIE BOWE

Rosemarie Bowe married actor Robert Stack five decades ago, thus ending her career. Prominent good looks had instantly made her a natural choice for the extravagant Technicolor musicals of the 1950s. She reached her pinnacle playing the lead in 'The Golden Mistress' (1954). The movie was shot on location in Haiti at the scared ruins of Christopher's San Souci and the Citadel. *'The story line was totally politically incorrect,'* said Bowe *'and really was nothing more than a vehicle to show me in various stages of undress'*. Today she resides in Los Angeles.

Top Three Films:
'The Mistress' (1954)
'Adventures of Hajji Baba' (1954)
'The Big Bluff' (1955)

PAULA RAYMOND

Paula Raymond made her featured debut riding the range opposite Kenne Duncan in 'Powder River Gunfire' (1948). A starlet at Columbia Studios, Raymond then moved to MGM where she was given star treatment. *'I met Louis B Mayer once,'* she said. *'He told me that my teeth were too straight and wanted to make them look crooked'.* Mayer quickly forgot all about Paula Raymond and what's more her teeth. Raymond moved from screen to television working mainly in westerns. Her career ended abruptly in 1962 when she was severely injured in a car crash. She sufficiently recovered to make a comeback during the 1970s.

Top Three Films:
'Devil's Doorway' (1950)
'Duchess of Idaho' (1950)
'The Gun That Won the West' (1955)

JACQUELINE LOUGHERY

Jacqueline Loughery became the first 'Miss USA' in 1952. That same year she married and promptly divorced singer, Guy Mitchell. Despite obtaining 'bit' parts in such movies as 'Veils of Baghdad' (1953), by the end of the decade, she was primarily just featured on the covers of glossy fashion magazines. However, her brief screen career ran to the 1970s, predominantly with television work. She lives in Encino, California.

Top Three Films:
'Abbott and Costello Go to Mars' (1953)
'The Naked Street' (1955)
'The Hot Angel' (1958)

THREE STARLETS OF THE GOLDEN AGE: ROSEMARIE BOWE (L), PAULA RAYMOND (C) AND JACQUELINE LOUGHERY (R)

TERRY MOORE

Glamour-girl, Terry Moore, has featured in numerous films from the 1940s, right through until the present day. Columbia Studio mogul, Harry Cohn, signed her up in 1948, changing her name from the Swedish Helen Luella Koford to the Irish Terry Moore. She's probably best known for her role in 'Mighty Joe Young' (1949), and earned an Oscar nomination for her excellent performance in 'Come Back, Little Sheba' (1952). Moore made headlines in the late 70s, claiming that she'd married millionaire Howard Hughes in 1949, having been introduced to him over dinner - a year previously - at the Beverly Wilshire Hotel. A romantic wedding ceremony was said to have taken place *"under the stars"* at the top of Mulholland Drive, Los Angeles. In 1983, Moore won a seven-year legal battle to be acknowledged as Hughes' widow. Following that, she then turned her hand to becoming a writer/producer on 'Beverly Hills Brats' (1989), starring Charlie Sheen and Ruby Keeler. She is a neighbour of the Reagan's in Bel Air, Los Angeles.

Top Three Films:
'Mighty Joe Black' (1949)
'Come Back, Little Sheba' (1952)
'Man on a Tightrope' (1952)

'BURGER OFF!' TERRY MOORE SNAPS BACK AT FRANK WORTH

THE YOUNG AND THE RECKLESS

JAMES DEAN

James Dean's persona has remained the subject of global speculation since the fateful car crash outside Palo Robles, California (on September 30 1955), which killed him at the tragically young age of twenty-four. Documentaries, books and now a recently rumoured up-coming Hollywood movie, all claim to take a different angle on the man behind the legend, debating his sexual proclivities and his supposed death wish. His first appearances were on the small screen in commercials and live dramas, including a stunt tester on 'Beat the Clock'. Dean obtained 'bit' parts in several films before moving to New York, where he gained notice (and the attention of director Elia Kazan) for his work in two plays, 'The Immoralist' and 'See the Jaguar'. After returning to the West Coast, the ruggedly handsome Dean played three lead roles in just over a year, displaying the astonishing versatility and force of a gifted new star. His self-assured persona, the brooding loner streak, rebellious image and angst-ridden grimace all struck a cord with teenagers across the world. Young and gifted, Dean was successful enough to be able to pick his own roles. He played Cal Trask in 'East of Eden', Jim Stark in 'Rebel Without a Cause' (both 1955) and the embittered oil tycoon, Jett Rink, in 'Giant' (1956). As with other legends who have died young, James Dean's fame was to be eternally enhanced by the tragedy of his brief but glittering 206 days of movie stardom.

Top Three Films:
'East of Eden' (1955)
'Rebel Without a Cause' (1955)
'Giant' (1956)

SCREEN REBEL JAMES DEAN ON THE SET OF 'GIANT' (1956)

JAMES DEAN

'I was invited onto the set of 'Giant' (1956) in Texas. Jimmy Dean was playing with a lasso. Trying to get his technique perfected. I said 'Oh anyone can do that, it's easy.' Jimmy looked me in the eye and said, 'Oh really Frank! Well if it is so easy let me see you try.' I made an ass of myself and everyone laughed at me. You know what? Jimmy took me aside after lunch and spent thirty-five minutes teaching me how to do it. We were an hour late getting back on set but he wouldn't return until I'd learnt how. That was the kinda guy Jimmy was.'

Frank Worth
(1988)

JAMES DEAN, AT THE RACETRACK

MARLON BRANDO

'Hollywood is a small town. When you go out and buy a house with a swimming pool, drive a caddy convertible, or go to Ciro's or The Mocambo, they don't like it. When you don't kow-tow to the powers of the town, they hate you. I am trying to do just two things – act, and live the way I want to live. Because I refuse to fall into the Hollywood mould, people think I'm a bum and a slob. Well, so be it! I've got nothing against Hollywood. But it is a business, and when you've made enough loot, the thing to do is pull out.'

Marlon Brando
That Guy Brando
(1955)

MARLON BRANDO AFTER WINNING THE BEST ACTOR OSCAR FOR 'ON THE WATERFRONT' (1954)

DENNIS HOPPER

The multi-faceted actor, director, producer and screenwriter Dennis Hopper, was often compared to James Dean. In fact, the pair were great friends and it was Dean who got Hopper his first screen break, eventually working together on 'Rebel Without a Cause' (1955) and 'Giant' (1956). Hopper admits that he spent the following decade in a drug-filled stupor, with the director Henry Hathaway labelling him 'completely uncontrollable'. Then came 'Easy Rider' (1969). It was a box-office and critical sensation. Hopper's 1970 marriage to Michelle Phillips lasted less than a week. He faltered badly, on and off screen, and in 1971, was arrested for partying stark naked in a Los Angeles park. Running on a high, Hopper then directed 'The Last Movie' (1969). It proved too offbeat for a mainstream audience and left him isolated by the establishment. Back on drugs, he appeared completely 'blotto' while making both Wim Wenders 'The American Friend' (1977) and 'Apocalypse Now' (1979). By the 1980s, Hopper had cleaned up and subsequently dished out a remarkable performance as the psychotic Frank Booth in David Lynch's 'Blue Velvet' (1986). Seven years on, he played Christian Slater's father in 'True Romance' (1993). More recently the volatile star added kudos to the sensational television series '24', playing the villain Victor Dreasen.

Top Three Films:
'Giant' (1956)
'Easy Rider' (1969)
'Blue Velvet' (1986)

DENNIS HOPPER AT MUSSO AND FRANK'S GRILL ON HOLLYWOOD BOULEVARD

ROBERT WAGNER

Nicknamed 'The Brylcreem Kid', Robert Wagner's love life was infamous. He dated Debbie Reynolds before marrying Natalie Wood. Hollywood trumpeted their marriage as *'The most glittering union of the 20th century'* but it faltered. As a young man under contract to 20th Century-Fox, Wagner was cast by Darryl F. Zanuck in 'With a Song in My Heart' (1952). Although the part lasted a scant minute, his performance as a crippled soldier responding to the song of Susan Hayward found an immediate reaction with the public. Spencer Tracy spotted Wagner in 'Beneath the Twelve Mile Reef' (1953) and requested him for the role of his son in 'Broken Lance' (1954). Tracy was so impressed that he then cast him as his brother in 'The Mountain' (1956). Although he had a number of good credits under his belt, Wagner's career was usually overshadowed by the more obvious heart throbs, Marlon Brando and Paul Newman. Distraught at the end of his marriage to Natalie Wood, he travelled to Europe to make 'The Longest Day' (1962), returning to Hollywood to re-marry her in 1972. The union lasted until her death. Wagner later scored a hit with his role opposite Stefanie Powers in 'Hart to Hart'. Ten years later he married actress Jill St. John, a friend since their days together at Fox. Still popular today, Mike Myers wrote the role of Number Two, the henchman of Dr. Evil in 'Austin Powers: International Man of Mystery' (1997), especially for Wagner, reprising the role in 'Austin Powers: The Spy Who Shagged Me' (1999) and 'Goldmember' (2002).

Top Three Films:
'Titanic' (1953)
'The Longest Day' (1962)
'Austin Powers: The Spy Who Shagged Me' (1999)

NATALIE WOOD

Fame touched Natalie Wood at a very early age. She enjoyed a career that spanned over forty years, making almost fifty movies and earning three Academy Award nominations. Yet the dark-eyed beauty would later comment that far from being overjoyed with her screen career, she was often withdrawn, frustrated and had always been desperate for a normal childhood. In 1955, Life magazine called her 'The Most Beautiful Teenager in America'. The Hollywood studios tried to manufacture her love life but in truth, she had already fallen for the young actor and playboy Robert Wagner, marrying him in 1957. The following decade established her reputation with roles like Maria in 'West Side Story' (1961). Despite her divorce and later remarriage to Robert Wagner, at this juncture, Wood's career had slowed down dramatically. She made her final film, 'Brainstorm' in 1981 starring Christopher Walken. Wood died in a boating accident in 1981.

Top Three Films:
'Rebel Without a Cause' (1955)
'The Searchers' (1956)
'West Side Story' (1961)

ROBERT WAGNER SHOWS HE IS THE TOAST OF TINSEL TOWN WITH WIFE NATALIE WOOD

ROCK HUDSON

Today, Rock Hudson is talked about as an 'A'-list actor, having appeared in many low-budget Universal-International films in the early 1950s. His breakthrough role came with the 1954 release 'Magnificent Obsession' in which he starred opposite Jane Wyman. Born in Winnetka, Illinois in 1925, under his real name of Roy Scherer Jr., Hudson failed to obtain parts in school plays because he could never remember his lines. After high school he was a postal employee and during WWII served as a Navy airplane mechanic. After the war he found work as a truck driver. In 1948, a chance meeting with a Hollywood agent, Henry Wilson, gave Hudson a leg-up in the business. Impressed by his stature and good looks, Wilson renamed the young man Rock Hudson, sent him to acting school and had him cap his teeth. Hudson landed his first film role in the 1948 movie 'Fighter Squadron' and in 1949, signed with Universal-International who gave him small roles in low-budget pictures, including the film noir thriller 'Undertow' (1949). The 60s revealed Hudson's talent for comedy in a series of Doris Day pictures. Over the years, he was romantically linked to a bevy of Hollywood starlets, marrying just once in 1955 to actress Phyllis Gates. They divorced three years later. In fact Rock Hudson had gone to great lengths to hide his homosexuality throughout his career. In July 1985, he announced that he was suffering from AIDS. Whilst Hudson was performing the role of suave horse breeder, Daniel Reece, in the American TV drama 'Dynasty', the virus had become lethally entrenched. Before long, an ailing and shockingly gaunt Hudson suffered memory loss and was forced to use cue cards. He also had difficulty speaking. He passed away on October 2 1985, at the age of 59.

Top Three Films:
'Magnificent Obsession' (1954)
'Giant' (1956)
'Pillow Talk' (1958)

ROCK HUDSON PRACTISES HIS LASSO SKILLS ON THE SET OF 'GIANT' (1956)

MARILYN MONROE

American actress Ruth Hall has been in films since the late 1920s. She is best remembered for her ingénue stint in the Marx Brothers 'Monkey Business' (1931). Hall married cinematographer Lee Garmes the following year. She made something of a comeback during the 1950s, gaining a small part in 'How to Marry a Millionaire' (1953).

'The girls on that movie were simply gorgeous. Well I mean Marilyn became the most recognisable face in the world. The movie was basically about three New York models that move into a Manhattan penthouse apartment and set out to find eligible millionaire bachelors to marry. I hadn't realised that your man Worth and Marilyn were friendly. I just knew him as the guy who shot Monroe, Lauren Bacall and Betty Grable between takes. Oh and me...!'

Ruth Hall
(2002)

MARILYN MONROE TAKES A MOMENT BEFORE HER NEXT SCENE IN 'HOW TO MARRY A MILLIONAIRE' (1953)

'GIANT' (1956)

Jane Withers was one of Hollywood's brightest child stars, second only to Shirley Temple at 20th Century-Fox. She survived her teens to enjoy a long and prosperous career, still continuing today.

'I remember how excited I was to have been given a part in 'Giant' (1956) and the privilege of working with the extraordinary cast that included Rock Hudson and Elizabeth Taylor. I knew Rock well. He had a delicious sense of humour. Liz, I didn't know, but we eventually became friends. Then there was Carroll Baker, Rod Taylor, Mercedes McCambridge, Noreen Nash and of course James Dean. He was shy and on the first day of shooting sort of mumbled to me a 'Hello.' I let Jimmy have his space. He was one of those extraordinary phenomena's that occurs only once. His star shone brighter than any of us, then crashed and burned, but will glow for ever more'.

Jane Withers
(2002)

A SEQUENCE OF IMAGES TAKEN BY FRANK WORTH ON THE SET OF 'GIANT' (1956)

TAB HUNTER

With his athletic build, blonde hair and blue eyes, Tab Hunter was quickly snapped-up by Hollywood film studios during the 1950s. A Warner Bros. contract firmly under his belt, Hunter was one of the last products of the studio system. He was born Arthur Andrew Gelien in 1931 in New York City. During his early teens and a keen swimmer, Hunter joined the Coast Guard (he lied claiming he was eighteen). It was during this time that the acting bug, which he'd sought to help overcome his timidity, bit him hard. He appeared in a series of sea and surf films as the glamorous all-American boy. The 1952 release 'Island of Desire' proved to be Hunter's big break and he was soon on his way to stardom. In the first half of the 50s, he made a few pictures including 'Return to Treasure Island' (1954) before signing with Warner Bros. During his tenure, Hunter started a successful pop career, first recording for the Dot label and scoring a top-ten hit with 'Young Love' in 1957. Later, he recorded for Warner Bros. when it established its own record label. During the late 1970s and early 80s, Tab Hunter moved further into television, portraying a coke-snorting lothario in John Waters' 'Polyester' (1981). Four years later, he appeared in the wonderfully camp 'Lust in the Dust' (1985), a film that he also produced. Now in his seventies and still sporting handsome features, Tab Hunter is hard at work. He has co-written a screenplay for a new comedy, 'Mother of the Bride', for which he will also serve as producer. He lives in Southern California.

Top Three Films:
'That Kind of Woman' (1959)
'Operation Bikini' (1963)
'Ride the Wild Surf' (1964)

NATALIE WOOD AND TAB HUNTER ANSWER QUESTIONS ON THEIR NEW RELATIONSHIP FOR HEDDA HOPPER'S TV SHOW

MARRIED HOLLYWOOD STYLE

LAUREN BACALL

Betty Joan Perke was born on September 16 1924. She originally wanted to be a dancer but then switched to acting classes at the American Academy of Dramatic Arts in New York. Once out of school the tall, gangly nineteen-year-old started modelling, notably for 'Harpers Bazaar' magazine. It was Howard Hawks's wife who spotted her, and taking a picture to her husband, urged him that this was the girl with 'The Look'. As a result, the newly christened Lauren Bacall was given a part as Marie Browning in 'To Have and To Have Not' (1944), starring Humphrey Bogart. The real-life off screen chemistry helped spice-up publicity for the film. Bogart and Bacall married in 1945. Her trademark deep sexy voice and arched eyebrows beautifully served the film noir in which she appeared. Both went on to star in several films together, although Bacall received only second billing in 'The Big Sleep' (1946). Her role in the movie 'Bright Leaf' (1950) was notable - her first without Bogart. Three years later she appeared as Schatze Page in 'How to Marry a Millionaire' (1953). Shortly after Bogart had died from cancer in 1957, Bacall announced that she and Frank Sinatra were to be married. When Sinatra backed out, she then married Jason Robards instead. As well as her film roles, Bacall was a sensation on Broadway. Despite several breaks during her career, this iconic beauty is still as active as active as ever.

Top Three Films:

'To Have or Have Not' (1944)
'The Big Sleep' (1946)
'Key Largo' (1948)

THE ULTIMATE HOLLYWOOD ODD COUPLE, BOGART AND BACALL

ELIZABETH TAYLOR

'The kids at Metro-Goldwyn-Mayer were so close, or was it simply publicity? Whatever the reason Elizabeth Taylor was bridesmaid for Jane Powell for her first marriage and Powell was bridesmaid for Taylor at her first marriage. It really was incestuous'.

Anonymous
(2002)

ELIZABETH TAYLOR ON HER WEDDING DAY IN BEVERLY HILLS. THE GROOM IS CONRAD 'NICKY' HILTON

CARY GRANT

If one had to choose a single word to describe Cary Grant, actor and heart throb, it would undoubtedly be 'smooth'. Two important factors separate Cary Grant from all other leading men – his sheer durability and an unerring gift for light comedy. Grant began life as Archibald Leach in Bristol, England in 1904. By 1921, he'd gone to America with a British repertory company. When the group packed to leave, Grant decided to stay and take his chances, working in vaudeville before switching to musical comedy. He was spotted by an Arthur Hammerstein talent scout, who offered him a juvenile lead in a new musical play, 'Golden Dawn'. He went on to make a string of unspectacular movies before Mae West entered his life, giving him the lead in 'She Done Him Wrong' (1933). The film was a box office smash, establishing Grant as a star. Two years later, he married actress Virginia Cherrill. Until then he had been sharing a one-bedroom apartment in Los Angeles with Randolph Scott. After he and Paramount parted company, Grant decided to freelance, making such memorable movies as 'Bringing Up Baby' and 'Holiday' (both 1938). The following decade united him with Alfred Hitchcock who was, like him, an expatriate Englishman. His first Hitchcock movie was 'Suspicion' (1941), though he went on to make a further three movies with the inimitable director. For the remaining years, Grant appeared only sporadically on screen. He died in November 1987 of a stroke, just one hour after giving a lecture on his extraordinary career, to a capacity crowd in Davenport, Iowa.

Top Three Films:
'Bringing Up Baby' (1938)
'Suspicion' (1941)
'North by Northwest' (1959)

BETSY DRAKE

Betsy Drake became Cary Grant's third wife on Christmas Day 1949, after meeting him on the set of her debut movie 'Every Girl Should Marry' (1948). The film is about a determined girl's quest to find, trap and marry the perfect man. Drake's stay in Hollywood was brief. She was often miscast or placed in dire pictures, notably 'Dancing in the Dark' (1949). In 1956, while Grant was away filming, Drake and actress Ruth Roman decided to take a vacation aboard the luxury liner Andrea Doria. Tragedy struck almost immediately. Mentioned by historians in the same breath as the Titanic, the sinking of the Andrea Doria on July 25 1956 was the worst passenger ship sea collision in history. Both she and Roman survived. The former Mrs. Cary Grant resides in Southern California.

Top Three Films:
'Pretty Baby' (1950)
'The Second Woman' (1951)
'Intent to Kill' (1958)

CARY GRANT AND HIS THIRD WIFE, BETSY DRAKE AT THE PREMIERE OF 'REAR WINDOW' (1954)

FRANK SINATRA

Sinatra, famously dubbed 'The Voice' and later 'Ol' Blue Eyes', was blessed with an extraordinary talent that propelled popular song into an art form. He was widely held to be the greatest singer in American pop history and one of the most successful entertainers of the twentieth century. He arrived in New York in 1930 intent on being a singer and within twelve years he had become the idol of the 'bobby sockers', defining the sort of mass hysteria that later greeted The Beatles. His show business career spanned fifty years, comprising of recordings, film and television appearances, as well as countless performances in nightclubs and major arenas. Sinatra's screen career flourished during the era of the movie musical, but when they went into decline so did Sinatra. It was his extraordinary Oscar winning portrayal of the feisty misfit soldier Maggio in 'From Here to Eternity' (1953), that put his career back on track. On a deeper level, Sinatra's public image touched many aspects of American cultural life. He was a top box office draw for nearly a decade, most notably as the leader of 'The Rat Pack', a hard-drinking, high-living clique. For millions, his ascent from humble Italian-American roots in Hoboken, New Jersey, was an inspirational symbol of immigrant achievement. At the end of his career, his annual income was estimated to be tens of millions of dollars. For decades, his private life, with its many romances, feuds, brawls and shady associations with mobsters, was grist for the gossip mill. But Sinatra also had a reputation for spontaneous generosity, for helping fledging singers and for supporting friends in need - including paying for all Ava Gardner's medical bills (the couple's tempestuous marriage lasted between 1951-1957). In 1976 he married for the fourth time, to Barbara Blakely Marx. In 1989, Sinatra toured the world with Sammy Davis Jr. and Liza Minnelli in a concert promoted as 'The Ultimate Event'. It was one of the grander bills in a rigorous touring schedule that he maintained into his late 70's. Sinatra died on May 14 1998.

Top Three Films:
'High Society' (1956)
'Pal Joey' (1957)
'Ocean's Eleven' (1960)

FRANK SINATRA AND SECOND WIFE, AVA GARDNER, MADE A SENSATIONAL COUPLE

HARRY JAMES

Harry James became one of the premiere Big Band leaders during the 1940s. He had been blowing the trumpet since the age of twelve, joining the Christy Brothers Circus band in the following year. In 1936 James joined Ben Pollack's band and then led the brass section of Benny Goodman's orchestra. In 1935, he married the singer Louise Tobin, but divorced her in 1943 to walk WWII pin-up Betty Grable down the aisle instead. She introduced him to her glitzy Hollywood set, increasing his profile. James became a favourite of dance lovers and jazz enthusiasts with his own particular style of swing. His version of 'You Made Me Love You' became a huge hit during the war years. James was renowned for spotting talent. While he was playing at a gig in New Jersey, he spotted a young waiter who showed promise - the boy was none other than Frank Sinatra! Harry James died of lymphatic cancer on July 5 1983.

Top Three Films:
'Springtime in the Rookies' (1942)
'Syncopation' (1942)
'On Our Merry Way' (1948)

AL JOLSON

Al Jolson was born Asa Yoelson in St. Petersburg in 1886. His Jewish parents wanted their son to become a cantor in a synagogue. Jolson had other ideas. He began his career with a circus, was promoted to café entertainer and then formed a vaudeville act with his brother. Jolson headed to the West Coast in 1923, later establishing himself as an actor in Hollywood. It was he who was responsible for the prophetic ad lib 'You ain't heard nothing yet' in 'The Jazz Singer' (1927), a movie that single handily opened the 'talkie' floodgates. He was requested to play himself in 'The Al Jolson Story' (1946), but then turned down the offer. The part went to Larry Parks and confirmed Jolson's place in movie star history. His third wife was actress Ruby Keeler. Jolson died of a heart attack in October 1950.

Top Three Films:
'The Jazz Singer' (1927)
'The Singing Fool' (1928)
'The Singing Kid' (1936)

AL JOLSON AND HARRY JAMES SNEAK A PEEK OVER BETTY GRABLE'S SHOULDER

JANET LEIGH

Sheer chance brought Janet Leigh - a student of music and psychology at the College of the Pacific - to the attention of MGM in 1946. Veteran actress, Norma Shearer spotted her portrait at the ski lodge where Leigh's parents worked in Northern California and took it to the studio. This led to a screen test and a subsequent starring role in 'The Romance of Rosy Ridge' (1947). MGM was looking for a young naive country girl and Janet filled the bill perfectly. Leigh played routine ingenués opposite Errol Flynn, James Stewart and Gary Cooper. With an aptitude for comedy, she played the title role in 'My Sister Eileen' (1955) opposite Betty Garrett and Jack Lemmon, and then also played the lead in the film noir thriller 'Touch of Evil' (1955). Leigh will always be most associated with Hitchcock's masterful movie 'Psycho' (1960), where she takes perhaps the most famous (and unforgettable) shower in movie history! Despite her watery and rather premature death in the picture, Leigh was still nominated for an Academy Award and received a Golden Globe. From 1951-1962, Leigh was married to Tony Curtis. Their daughter is actress Jamie Lee Curtis. She lives today in Beverly Hills, California.

Top Three Films:
'The Romance of Rosy Ridge' (1947)
'Little Women' (1949)
'Psycho' (1960)

TONY CURTIS

A veteran of some 130 movies, Tony Curtis was born in the Bronx and began his career in 1949. He debuted in the theatre initially using the name James Curtis, and then Anthony, before finally opting for Tony. He always tried to work across the genres to avoid being typecast. In the comedy spectrum he excelled in such classics as 'Some Like It Hot' (1959) and 'Goodbye Charlie' (1964), but was also admired in adventure pictures such as 'The Vikings' (1958). His talent stretched to more complex and psychological roles as seen in 'The Boston Strangler' (1968). Curtis was always a wow with the girls. *"I ran around with a lump in my pants"*, he said. *"I chased all the girls. This is what I reflected on the screen. There wasn't anything deeper or less deep than that."* He lives in Southern California.

Top Three Films:
'The Defiant Ones' (1958)
'Some Like It Hot' (1959)
'Spartacus' (1960)

JUMPING FOR JOY - NEWLY WEDS TONY CURTIS AND JANET LEIGH

ROY ROGERS

Roy Rogers was called 'The King of the Cowboys' during his long career as a folksy singing hero of movies and television. He started out working in a shoe factory during the Depression Era and then as a fruit picker. However, his passion for singing and guitar led him to radio. He became an original member of the cowboy singing group 'The Sons of the Pioneers', and in 1937, he signed up with Republic Pictures, replacing their departing star Gene Autry. Rogers starred in more than 80 westerns including classic titles 'The Arizona Kid' (1939) and 'In Old Cheyenne' (1941). He often co-starred with the toothless Gabby Hayes and cowgirl Dale Evans, later to be his wife. Rogers' famous horse was Trigger, a Palomino stallion with a flowing white mane, who became a favourite with fans. In the 1950s, Rogers launched the massively successful 'The Roy Rogers Show' on television. The theme song, the gentle and cheery 'Happy Trails to You', became one of the highest selling records in American history. Rogers was elected to the Country Music Hall of Fame twice. After Trigger's death, the horse was mounted and put on display at the Roy Rogers Museum in Victorville, California. The Roy Rogers chain of fast food restaurants first opened in 1968, earning Rogers and Evans a second fortune. Yet another career in real estate followed. Still popular, their museum is one of the biggest tourist attractions in Southern California. Rogers died on July 6 1998, four months prior to Gene Autry.

Top Three Films:
'Under Western Stars' (1938)
'Yellow Rose of Texas' (1944)
'Son of Paleface' (1952)

WESTERN HUSBAND AND WIFE TEAM, ROY ROGERS AND DALE EVANS

DALE EVANS

The actress, Dale Evans, dubbed 'Queen of the West', became the most famous of Hollywood's Western leading ladies, through her marriage to singing cowboy, Roy Rogers. Born Lucille Wood Smith, she was a gifted child student who by the age of eleven was studying alongside fifteen-year-old girls. Her parents were delighted, but Dale was withdrawn and spent her summer vacation bedridden and suffering from nervous exhaustion. She quit school the following term and at the age of fourteen, eloped with Thomas Frederick Fox, the boyfriend of an older classmate. The following year, she gave birth to a son Fredrick Fox Junior. The marriage ended in 1929, two months before her seventeenth birthday. She then headed to Memphis, Tennessee, where she persued her dream of becoming a singer. The early days were a struggle for Evans, but her determination to find work eventually paid off. She found herself singing and playing the piano for three separate radio stations. Joe Eaton at WHAS radio came up with the name Dale Evans. She quickly made the transition from radio to cinema, thanks largely to her pushy agent, Joe Rivkin. By the mid-thirties she was on a one-year contract at $400 a week. During WWII, Dale toured with the USO and The Hollywood Victory Committee. It was at one benefit that her future husband, Roy Rogers, entered her sphere. *"I remember turning to my escort, Charlie McCarthy and saying, "I want to meet Roy Rogers, he is my rising star!"* Herbert Yates, head of Republic Studios, decided that as she could ride a horse better than any other actress on contract, she'd be the perfect choice for his project to expand female leads in westerns. In 1944, Yates teamed her with Roy Rogers for 'The Cowboy and the Senorita', the first of their twenty-eight pictures together. Dale Evans died of congestive heart failure on February 7 2001 in Apple Valley, California.

Top Three Films:
'Casanova in Burlesque' (1943)
'The Cowboy and the Senorita' (1944)
'Don't Fence Me In' (1945)

'Roy was a naughty boy. He liked pretty women but also liked his home life, the kiddies and a wife. He met me while I was at Republic. I was in make-up when he came over and kissed me. I was shocked. Roy just laughed and said that I had a face that just had to be kissed. I cannot remember if we eventually slept together. However, I do remember seeing him naked except for those wonderful cowboy boots. Yes, Roy must have done it with his boots on!'

Judith Allen
(1995)

LEX BARKER

The handsome, blonde, muscular six-foot Adonis, Lex Barker was born into a wealthy family that thought little of performing artists. Therefore, in the early 1940s when Barker decided to drop out of Princeton to become an actor, his family practically disowned him. (Barker was a direct descendant of Roger Williams - the founder of Rhode Island - and of Sir William Henry Crichlow, historical Governor General of Barbados). He turned down a contract with 20th Century Fox, opting instead to enlist in the Armed Forces during film WWII. After the war, the talented Barker attempted to resume his acting career and began landing small film roles. However, he would have to wait until 1949 for stardom, when producer Sol Lesser selected him, after screening hundreds of actors to replace Johnny Weissmuller, for the title role in 'Tarzan's Magic Fountain'. 'Sexy Lexy' was an obvious choice, and went onto play the loin-clothed ape-man five times. He made more than 50 films across the world, including Brazil, Spain, Yugoslavia, Italy, Lebanon and France. In 1966, his massive popularity in Germany was recognised with the Bambi Award for Best Foreign Actor. In May 1973, he completed his last film 'Wo Alle Wege Enden' just days before a heart attack claimed his life aged fifty-four. His five wives include actresses Lana Turner and Arlene Dahl.

Top Three Films:

'Crossfire' (1947)
'Tarzan's Magic Fountain' (1949)
'La Dolce Vita' (1959)

MERVYN LE ROY (C) LEAVES LEX BARKER AND WIFE, LANA TURNER IN STITCHES

MICHAEL WILDING

The dashingly good-looking Michael Wilding oozed debonair charm, in spite of his own reservations about his acting ability. Wilding's fan base was huge, his lifestyle sophisticated and his four wives, including Margaret Leighton and Elizabeth Taylor - beautiful. Born in Westcliffe-on-Sea, Wilding was educated in Essex, and at seventeen embarked on a career as an artist. He discovered acting quite by chance making his debut in the Austrian film 'Pastorale' (1933). After a return to the theatre, a screen career beckoned again in the early 1940's, partnering Anna Neagle in a series of escapist dramas set among London's upper classes. His most important American film, 'Torch Song' (1953) partnered him with Joan Crawford. Wilding died after suffering a serious fall in London on July 8 1979.

Top Three Films:
'Tilly of Bloomsbury' (1940)
'The Countess of Curzon Street' (1947)
'Maytime in Mayfair' (1949)

ELIZABETH TAYLOR WITH HER DAPPER SECOND HUSBAND MICHAEL WILDING

STRIKE A POSE

NOREEN NASH

This brunette Hollywood starlet of the 1940s and 50s was born on April 4 1924 in Wenatchee, Washington. Arriving in the movie capital after gaining stage experience off-Broadway, she was placed under contract with MGM, only to be offered token roles playing beautiful mannequins and showgirls. Nash made her screen debut in the Judy Garland, Mickey Rooney musical comedy 'Girl Crazy' (1943). *"I was mesmerized by MGM,"* she said in 2002. *"The slogan there at the time was 'More Stars Than There Are In Heaven', and couldn't have been more true"*. After her MGM contract expired she decided to go freelance, playing the lead in 'B' movies and supporting roles in 'A' list films, notably as Lona Lane in 'Giant' (1956). Her husband is the actor James Whitmore and together, the couple are frequent visitors to film conventions and charity galas. Noreen's stepson, James Whitmore Jr. is also an actor. Nash and Whitmore live in Malibu, California.

Top Three Films:
'Assigned to Danger' (1948)
'Phantom From Outer Space' (1953)
'Giant' (1956)

THE SUBLIME NOREEN NASH POSES AT HOME IN HOLLYWOOD

ELIZABETH TAYLOR

'Louis B. Mayer and MGM created stars out of cellophane and newspapers. But all the stars were born and died more or less at the whim of Mayer, who was an absolute dictator of the studio - and a good deal of Hollywood to boot'.

Elizabeth Taylor
Movie Digest
(1973)

ELIZABETH TAYLOR PRACTISES HER LASSO SKILLS ON THE SET OF 'GIANT' (1956)

MARILYN MONROE

'If you've noticed in Hollywood where millions and billions of dollars have been made, there aren't any kind monuments or museums - and I don't call putting your footprint in Graumen's Chinese Theatre a monument'

Marilyn Monroe
Marilyn Monroe: In Her Own Words
(1983)

MARILYN MONROE DRAPES HERSELF ACROSS FRANK WORTH'S CAR DURING A 1953 PHOTO SHOOT

LORETTA YOUNG

Loretta Young was Hollywood's 'Steel Butterfly', a title given by her first husband actor Grant Withers, depicting her delicate appearance and awesome resilience. Energetic and photogenic, Loretta rose from the ranks of the 'bit' player to superstardom at 20th Century-Fox. She was one of four acting sisters, Sally Blane, Polly Ann and Georgiana Young, beginning her career working in silent pictures. Loretta waited until 1947 to receive her career boost by earning an Academy Award for 'The Farmers Daughter'. In 1953, she became the first woman of her calibre to host her own television series. This exposure brought a wider variety of roles, several Emmys and huge financial rewards. Loretta made her last appearance for the 'Hollywood' edition of Vanity Fair magazine in 1999. Between husbands, she had intense relationships with Spencer Tracy and Clark Gable. The latter was actually named, during the late 80s, as the father of Loretta's daughter, Judy. Young died in Los Angeles, California, on August 12 2000.

Top Three Films:
'Suez' (1938)
'The Bishops Wife' (1938)
'The Farmers Wife' (1947)

TYRONE POWER

Tyrone Power was one of the last studio-owned stars, his father having been a matinee idol of Broadway and silent movies. Power made his screen debut in 1932, a year after the death of his father. He had hoped to emulate his success, and to some degree, Power superseded his wildest expectations, becoming 20th Century Fox's top male star around 1937. However, he was constantly submerged in one colourless part after another. When leaving Fox in 1954, Power went through a run of films that, although not particularly outstanding, were improvements on his diet of drab costume dramas. He married the actress Annabella, his co-star from 'Suez' (1938) in 1939. The union lasted until 1946. Shortly before her death, Annabella said the split happened because of his bisexuality. Despite this, Power married Mexican actress Linda Christian in 1949. His best film during the 50s was 'Witness for the Prosecution' (1958). He collapsed and died in Spain while shooting 'Solomon and Sheba' (1959), with his third wife giving birth to a son just three months later. Tyrone Power Jr. II followed in the family's thespian footsteps and is also an actor.

Top Three Films:
'Suez' (1938)
'Blood and Sand' (1941)
'The Razors Edge' (1946)

SCREEN LEGEND LORETTA YOUNG DINES WITH 'SEUZ' (1938) CO-STAR, TYRONE POWER

FRANK SINATRA

'I managed to persuade the Ford motor company to loan me one of their brand spanking new Thunderbird cars for a photo shoot I'd planned with Frank Sinatra. He had agreed to this exclusive, which took us a morning to complete. Frank was having a ball, as he adored the car. So much so infact, that he rang Ford asking if he could buy the car. And they were only too pleased to oblige'.

Frank Worth
(1987)

FRANK SINATRA AT THE WHEEL OF A BORROWED FORD THUNDERBIRD. HE LIKED THE CAR SO MUCH, HE BOUGHT IT!

MARILYN MONROE

Dear Frank,
It was nice having you in me
Love Marilyn

A note from Marilyn Monroe to Frank Worth
Circa 1953

MARILYN MONROE OOZING JOYOUS SEX APPEAL

THE PIRATE

'The Pirate' (1948) is an exciting take on the old swashbuckler movies (with song and dance numbers to boot). Consequently it has the adventurous, romantic elements of the old films combined with hilarious parody. The director, Vincente Minnelli, was accused of spending too much on the lavish sets and little or no detail to the cast and content. In 1992 actress Jean Dean recalled, *'I thought the film was troubled from the start. The outlandish sets were paid for at the expense of the film. The pairing of the exuberant Gene Kelly and unstable Judy Garland was all wrong. Judy became increasingly impossible as the weeks went on. The poor darling was often drunk and very bad mannered. The trouble was that everyone loved her so and she just couldn't see it. We spent days hanging around the set or escaping to practise our routines as Vincente tried to get Judy dried out'*. Despite this, 'The Pirate' (1948) was credited as one of the best movies of the year.

REHEARSALS FOR 'THE PIRATE' (1948)

MARILYN MONROE

'There isn't a decent man in Hollywood. They're all out for one thing. They don't even bother romancing you. Some of them are good-looking and they think that's enough. The hell with that'.

Marilyn Monroe
(1960)

MARILYN MONROE GETS READY TO PITCH AT THE BALL GAME

HOLLYWOOD AT HOME

JAMES DEAN

'The first time I met James Dean was on the parking lot of Schwabs pharmacy. I then found out he was an actor. I didn't know much about him then, but he was a nice guy, a nice kid who looked like a struggling actor trying to make his way. One day I said to him, 'I'm doing a movie star layout for a fan magazine, why don't you come along and when I am shooting a star, try and shuffle into the picture.' He was very shy and sheepish and pleased I'd asked him, but said, 'No.' Sometime later I was invited to a screening of 'East of Eden'. I was late getting there and so missed all the credits, only catching the name of the director. It started and then up there on the screen was Jimmy Dean. 'Oh my God,' I thought, he got himself a bit part. Five minutes later and he was the star. I could not believe it. The minute the picture finished I ran to a phone and I called him up. 'You dirty rotten fink,' I said, 'How could you do this to me, you are a star!'

Frank Worth
(1988)

A DEXTEROUS JAMES DEAN TAKES A PEE AND A CALL

RITA HAYWORTH

She was born Margarita Carmen Cansino on October 17 1918 and at the age of three, was learning to dance as a member of 'The Dancing Cansinos'. Her friend, the Mexican star Lupita Tovar, suggested she try her luck in movies. Hayworth subsequently headed west to Hollywood, shortening her name to Rita and appearing as a dancer in 'Dante's Inferno' (1935). By 1937, she'd taken on her mother's maiden name - Hayworth. Rita's break came with prominent roles in 'Only Angels Have Wings' (1939) and 'Blood and Sand' (1941) both became huge commercial successes. A new movie Love Goddess was born, although initially, Hayworth was timid and unassuming. This soon changed along with her appearance. She approved the raising of her hairline by electrolysis as well dying it red. Her new look - combined with luscious lips and a voice that was both soft and caressing - transformed Hayworth into a huge box office star. This was never more evident than as the innocent, misunderstood femme fatale in 'Gilda' (1946). Ironically, by the time of the film's release, Hayworth's career had begun to flop. Although she was still making movies, nothing approached the heights of her earlier work, added to which her several marriages had appeared to interrupt the flow of her career. She slipped from glamour girl to character actress, by the time she married and then divorced singer Dick Haymes. Momentarily, Hayworth's star shone again as ex-stripper Vera Simpson in 'Pal Joey' (1957). One reason for the downward spiral was the growth of television, but Rita had also been overtaken in the popularity stakes by husky blonde bombshell, Kim Novak. By the 70s, her work was primarily European-bound, and by the end of the decade, Hayworth's career was over. There was much concern over her health. Incoherent behaviour was blamed on an alcohol addiction, but it was not until 1980 that she was correctly diagnosed as suffering from Alzheimer's disease. In 1981, and almost helpless, Rita was cared for by her daughter Princess Yasmin Aga Khan until her death in 1987 at the age of 68 (Hayworth was married to the Aly Khan 1949-1951). Her second husband was Orson Welles.

Top Three Films:

'You Were Never Lovelier' (1942)
'Gilda' (1946)
'Pal Joey' (1957)

RITA HAYWORTH SHOWS THAT IT'S NOT JUST THE BOYS WHO PLAY WITH TRAIN SETS

RITA HAYWORTH

Frank Worth was just 17 when he photographed Rita Hayworth, both in the garden of her home and shopping on Hollywood Boulevard in December 1939. The images were never processed, lying in a small brown envelope at the bottom of a cardboard box for over sixty years.

RITA HAYWORTH CATCHING RAYS IN HER HOLLYWOOD GARDEN (1939)

PIER ANGELI

The Italian born Pier Angeli never truly achieved star status. Mostly forgotten today, she arrived in Hollywood during the 1950s but, despite much hype, was never given the sort of roles that helped catapult her contemporaries into becoming movie legends. On a romantic level however, things were a lot more colourful, and during her spell in the movie capital, Angeli bedded many Hollywood heartthrobs. Her greatest love was James Dean. Angeli and Dean met whilst he was making 'East of Eden' in 1955, and instantly fell in love. Onlookers suggested that her beauty and demure personality were irresistible to the notoriously promiscuous Dean. But despite their obvious mutual affection, her own mother, Dean's business manager and MGM (where she was under contract) quashed the union. The regrettable combination of a domineering matriarch, an unfulfilling career, a miscarriage and the loss of Dean, tragically instigated her four suicide attempts. By 1970 Angeli was becoming truly unstable and was also reportedly in debt. Offers of help came too late, and in 1971, aged 39, she overdosed on barbiturates. She left a son, Perry, from her marriage to singer Vic Damone.

Top Three Films:
'Theresa' (1951)
'The Flame and the Flesh' (1954)
'Somebody Up There Likes Me' (1956)

PIER ANGELI AND SON PLAY WITH THEIR NEW DOG, AMBER

MITZI GAYNOR

A leading lady of light musicals, the bright-eyed Mitzi Gaynor is best remembered for her lead in 'South Pacific' (1958). Whenever the mood takes her, the vivacious former child ballerina has been known to claim an impressive hereditary from Hungarian nobility, stating her birth name as Francesca Mitzi Marlene de Channey von Gerber. Both her mother and aunt were dancers, so it was expected that Gaynor might well follow suit. Making her debut as a toddler, Gaynor became a dancer at the Los Angeles Civic Light Opera. It was whilst playing the lead in 'Naughty Marietta' that she was chosen by 20th Century-Fox for 'My Blue Heaven' (1950). Fox thought of Gaynor as an ideal replacement for Betty Grable. She sang and danced her way through a string of musicals but lacked the same screen presence as Grable and, in 1954, was dropped. Gaynor married talent agent Jack Bean in the autumn of the same year and under his guidance, was catapulted to stardom as a stage and nightclub performer. Bean then successfully orchestrated a contract for his wife at Paramount Pictures. Her best work came when she was loaned to MGM for George Cukor's 'Les Girls' (1957), with Gene Kelly and Tania Elg. In 1958, she was tapped for the much sort-after role of Nellie Forbush in Joshua Logan's film version of Rodgers and Hammerstein's 'South Pacific'. Although a favourite amongst cinema goers, the critics panned the movie and the unfortunate Gaynor met with the brunt of their criticism. Her screen career was all but over by the 1960s. A decade on, she returned to headline in a television special. She currently resides in Beverly Hills.

Top Three Films:

'Anything Goes' (1954)
'Les Girls' (1957)
'South Pacific' (1958)

MITZI GAYNOR CHARMS FRANK WORTH

ELIZABETH TAYLOR

'Well, Elizabeth was just a kid when I photographed her for an 'At Home' shoot. She was so polite, constantly saying please and thank you and asking if she looked alright through the lens. The truth was Elizabeth looked magnificent'.

Frank Worth
(1987)

ELIZABETH TAYLOR FRESHENS UP AT HER PARENTS HOLLYWOOD HOME

ON THE TOWN

WILLIAM HOLDEN

Barbara Stanwyck saw a young William Holden hanging around the back lot of Paramount Pictures. She liked his looks and suggested to director Rouben Mamoulian that he be cast as the musically minded boy who becomes a prizefighter, in 'Golden Boy' (1939). Holden made his mark and the pair became life-long friends. Holden became one of the film industry's most dependable leading men, giving an awesome performance as the journalist-gigolo in 'Sunset Boulevard' (1950) with Gloria Swanson. 'Born Yesterday' (1950) was a vehicle for his comic abilities, showing him in the role of a teacher given the impossible task of refining a junk dealer's wife (Judy Holliday). A Best Actor Oscar honoured his portrayal of a prisoner-of-war in 'Stalag 17' (1956). The 1960s offered little to stretch Holden's talent, except perhaps for the lead in Sam Peckinpah's 'The Wild Bunch' (1969). Later, his role as a conscientious newsman in 'Network' (1976) earned him a new legion of fans. A committed wildlife conservationist, Holden always aimed to spend at least six months a year at his Mount Kenya Safari Club ranch, often accompanied by his actress partner, Stefanie Powers. In April 1981, he died after falling and hitting his head on the marble fireplace at his Los Angeles apartment.

Top Three Films:
'Sunset Boulevard' (1950)
'Born Yesterday' (1950)
'Stalag 17' (1953)

JANE WYMAN

Jane Wyman was nominated no less than four times for Best Actress Oscars, before becoming a Golden Globe winner for her role in the daytime soap opera 'Falcon Crest', during the 1980s. She started her career during the early 30s in the chorus line of Busby Berkeley musicals. By the next decade, she'd moved into supporting roles. Wyman married fellow actor Ronald Reagan in 1940. Her first role of note was as Helen St. James, the long-suffering girlfriend of Ray Milland in 'The Lost Weekend' (1945), followed by the role of Ma Baxter, Gregory Peck's forbearing spouse, in 'The Yearning' (1946). Wyman won an Oscar two years later as the deaf mute in 'Johnny Belinda' (1948). The same year she and Reagan were divorced. She reached her peak in Douglas Sirk's 'Magnificent Obsession' (1954) and 'All That Heaven Allows' (1955), after which she virtually retired. Wyman lives in Rancho Mirage, California.

Top Three Films:
'Lost Weekend' (1945)
'The Yearning' (1946)
'Johnny Belinda' (1948)

WILLIAM HOLDEN (L), JANE WYMAN AND CARY GRANT DINING OUT AT THE COCONUT GROVE

RONALD REAGAN

The 40th President of the United States (1981-1989) graduated from Eureka College in 1932. He was a sports announcer on local radio in Des Moines, Iowa, eventually becoming the regular host for the Chicago Club games. Popularly known as 'Dutch', actress Joy Hodges was largely responsible for launching his screen career in 1937, by persuading Universal Pictures to give him a screen test. Reagan was unsuccessful. Hodges points to the reason being Reagan's thick-rimmed glasses. *'No leading man wore anything quite as ugly'* she said. Next time round and spectacle free, Reagan was successful. Just over six feet tall, handsome with wavy hair and broad shoulders, the studio groomed him for stardom. His first major movie was opposite Bette Davis in 'Dark Victory' (1939). Davis commented *'I could hardly believe it when 'Dutch', the boy we all knew as silly little Ronnie, became President'.* After War duty, Reagan was reduced to more mediocre support roles. To counter balance this, he became heavily involved in union activities. He was the President of the Screen Actors' Guild from 1947-1952 and again from 1959-1960. 'B' movie actress Nancy Davis came into his life in 1950, and two years later, they married with their close friend William Holden as best man. Nancy Reagan saw great potential in her husband. She was a staunch anti-communist and under her influence, he embraced conservatism, moving from Democrat to Republican. He supported Barry Goldwater for President in 1964, the year of his final movie. Two years later, he became governor of California, supported by a bevy of Hollywood friends including Billie Dove, Irene Dunne, Ginger Rogers and Fred MacMurray. Some of whom later served as advisors on his 'Kitchen Cabinet'. Joy Hodges was one such friend and at a White House gala dinner in 1987, she turned to President Gorbachev and said *'Gorby take down that darn Berlin Wall'* – and he did. Reagan won his party's candidacy in 1980 and was elected President both in 1980 and 1984, proving during his two terms, that he was a much better actor than anyone had ever suspected. Reagan had two children with his first wife, Jane Wyman and two more with Nancy Reagan. During the 90s, Reagan was diagnosed with Alzheimer's disease. Joking he said, *'There's one good thing about Alzheimer's. You're always meeting new people!'*

Top Three Films:
'Dark Victory' (1939)
'This is the Navy' (1943)
'Bedtime for Bonzo' (1951)

RONALD REAGAN (L) JOINS HIS WARNER BROS. CONTEMPORARIES PAT O'BRIEN (C) AND JAMES CAGNEY AT A HOLLYWOOD PARTY

JAYNE MANSFIELD

'Jayne and I were kinda friendly and I wanted to do something nice for her. I knew all the agents, all the press agents and the right people. But I didn't tell her that, I wanted to surprise her. My friend Burt Kaiser was making this film 'The Female Jungle' (1956). I got her sixth billing in it. She had a fling with Lawrence Tierney, then she ditched her husband Paul Mansfield and that's when we got together. I wanted to be her agent but a guy named Jim Byron beat me to it. I got her an invite to accompany me on a press junket for a Jane Russell picture called 'Underwater'. I took pictures of Jayne in the pool of our hotel and she looked wonderful. There have been sordid versions of how Jayne and I got close, all of them rubbish. They said that Matt James at RKO called me asking if I knew of any girls with big boobs. I never used that word. Why would I call something so beautiful 'Boobs'? To me a boob is a nut and there wasn't anything remotely nutty about Jayne.'

Frank Worth
(1987)

JAYNE MANSFIELD SMILES AT HER OLD FLAME FRANK WORTH

ZSA ZSA GABOR

Despite some interesting roles in films like 'Touch of Evil' (1958), little can compare to Zsa Zsa Gabor herself - the diamond-dazzling silver fox-clad Hungarian blonde bombshell. Her date of birth is somewhat murky, though she was born Sari Gabor in Budapest, the second daughter of society hostess Jolie Gabor. Zsa Zsa would go on to win the 1936 Miss Hungary beauty pageant and fulfil her mother's aspirations of becoming world famous. Between them, the Gabors notched-up over twenty husbands. Zsa Zsa was undoubtedly the most recognisable amongst them, but was beaten to the silver screen by her younger sister, Eva. Her biggest success was a star performance in John Huston's 'Moulin Rouge' (1952), although she is often fondly remembered by camp devotees for her role in 'Queen of Outer Space' (1958). Zsa Zsa also really came into her own on the chat show circuit. Always ready with a biting quip or torrid tale from her hedonistic past, she referred to everyone as *'Daarlink!'* Her marriage to Prince Frederick von Anhalt in 1986 bestowed her with the grand title of Princess Zsa Zsa von Anhalt, Duchess of Saxony. In 1990 she was convicted of slapping a Los Angeles police officer during a traffic dispute and spent several days in jail. After a spate of movie roles during the mid to late 90s, Zsa Zsa withdrew from the screen. The deaths of both sisters and her mother, sent her further into a retreat in her cavernous Bel Air mansion. She is thought to be in her early eighties and is a virtual recluse. She had only one child from her nine marriages, a daughter, Francesca, by Conrad 'Nicky' Hilton.

Top Three Films:
'Moulin Rouge' (1952)
'Queen of Outer Space' (1958)
'Touch of Evil' (1958)

ZSA ZSA GABOR WITH HER PUBLICIST RICHARD STRAILE IN HOLLYWOOD (1954)

MICKEY ROONEY

The former child star Mickey Rooney was born Joe Yule Junior in 1920. His family were well established on the vaudeville circuit and put their baby son on stage before he was a year old. His mother subsequently took Rooney to Hollywood where he landed his first film playing a midget in 'Not to be Trusted' (1926). Changing his name to Mickey McGuire he featured in almost one hundred short films. McGuire then became Rooney, and gave an extraordinary performance as Puck in 'A Midsummer Nights Dream' (1935). He reached the peak of his fame whilst under contract to MGM, playing the lead in fifteen highly successful 'Andy Hardy' movies, often accompanied by Cecilia Parker and Judy Garland. By the tail end of the 40s, the public had turned away from the pint-sized showman in favour of a new, younger breed of actor. He resurfaced during the 60s and again in 1979 when he and Ann Miller joined forces for the highly successful burlesque revue, 'Sugar Babies'. One of his eight wives was the actress Ava Gardner. In 1983, the Academy of Motion Pictures Arts and Sciences recognised Rooney's astounding contribution to the world of entertainment, by presenting him with an honorary Oscar. *'I'm so happy,'* he said. *'Why I could even kiss Louis B. Mayer!'*

Top Three Films:
'Boys Town' (1938)
'The Adventures of Huckleberry Finn' (1939)
'National Velvet' (1944)

A YOUTHFUL MARILYN MONROE AND HER DATE FOR THE EVENING, MICKEY ROONEY

CARL REINER

Carl Reiner joined up with the WPA Dramatic Workshop whilst in his late teens. Later, he worked with actor Maurice Evans' GI troupe in the South Pacific during WWII, after which he performed on-stage with several road companies and on Broadway. During the 1950s, Reiner worked as a co-writer and actor with Sid Caesar on 'Your Show of Shows.' In 1958, he published the semi-autobiographical novel, 'Enter Laughing', which he later adapted for both stage and screen. Unemployed in the early 60s, Reiner attempted to design a TV series as a vehicle for himself, but the pilot fell at the first hurdle. Undaunted, he went away, re-worked it and the hugely successful 'The Dick Van Dyke Show' sitcom was born, winning five Emmy Awards. He went onto receive a further six during his eclectic career, including a wonderfully funny cameo in 'The Thrill of it All' (1963), with Doris Day, James Garner and Zasu Pitts. As a director and writer, Carl Reiner helped launch stand-up comic Steve Martin in a spate of his films, including 'The Jerk' (1979) and 'The Man with Two Brains' (1983). His sons Rob and Lucas have both followed him into the world of movies.

Top Three Films:
'The Thrill of it All' (1963)
'A Guide for the Married Man' (1967)
'Ocean's Eleven' (2001)

CARL REINER HAS A FEW QUESTIONS TO PUT TO MARILYN MONROE

JAYNE MANSFIELD

'I liked to help people. People who I thought showed promise. I helped Rita, Marilyn and sought to help Jimmy Dean, and gave Jayne Mansfield a very important push early on in her career. She never forgot it and would try and seek me out whenever she attended a premiere or a party in order to give me her best look of the evening'.

Frank Worth on Jayne Mansfield
(1987)

JAYNE MANSFIELD AT THE CASINO (1956)

HEDDA HOPPER AND LOUELLA PARSONS

Once, there was a different Hollywood where high-powered producers, directors and stars weren't at the controls. The big studios were run by some of the most powerful men in Hollywood - Jack Warner, Louis B. Mayer, Harry Cohn, Irving Thalberg. But even these giants cowered before two women: Hedda Hopper and Louella Parsons, the two most powerful gossip columnists in American history. If Louella Parsons was known as the Bitch Goddess of a starlet's career, Hedda Hopper was often the Guardian Angel. However, because of the power of their columns - Louella's in the Hearst papers, Hedda's in the Los Angeles Times - they were a force to be reckoned with, whether dealing with an established name or not. Out of favour and you might as well get the bus back home, because their opinion could dictate a future no glitzier than waiting on tables, pumping gas, or walking the streets. Parsons ended her days in a nursing home, having retired some years before her death in 1972. Her passing went virtually unnoticed. By that time the industry had changed beyond recognition. Despite this, there were a few veterans who cynically hoped that her death had been the result of someone driving a stake through her heart. Hedda Hopper's career continued well after Parsons' had finished. She hosted her own successful gossip show on television, interviewing such diverse stars as Marion Davies and The Beatles. Hopper died on the eve of the Broadway revival of 'Gypsy', on February 1 1966.

Top Three Films:

'The Man Who Lost Himself' (1920)
'Don Juan' (1926)
'The Patsy' (1964)

RITA HAYWORTH AND HEDDA HOPPER (L) GOSSIP ABOUT STARS

KIRK DOUGLAS

Kirk Douglas, the dashing, dimple-chinned Hollywood actor, was born Issur Danielovitch Demsky to Russian immigrant parents in 1916. Having Americanised his name, Douglas attended the American Academy of Dramatic Arts. He graduated in 1941, making a few appearances on Broadway, before WWII interrupted his progress. Later Douglas resumed his stage career when his old classmate, Lauren Bacall, suggested he meet with the producer Hal B. Wallis. A screen test was made, resulting in his first leading role in 'The Strange Love of Martha Ivers' (1946), starring alongside Barbara Stanwyck and the sultry Lizabeth Scott. Douglas won rave reviews as Walter O'Neil and decided to remain in Hollywood, eventually becoming one of the industry's ultimate tough guys. He was cast in a number of thrillers and costume epics. One of his early movies and a personal favourite - 'I Walk Alone' (1948) - put him alongside close friend Burt Lancaster. In 1949, he was cast as tough boxer Midge Kelly, a role he played with superb aplomb, earning Douglas his first Academy Award. His characters, usually the victims of their own aggression, always seem to have an appealing depth. Kirk Douglas' career spans across six decades and although he suffered a debilitating stroke in 1995, it didn't rob him of his determination to work and devote his energies towards charity projects. His movie star son, Michael, is carrying on the Douglas acting dynasty, making his own legendary mark in Hollywood.

Top Three Films:

'The Bad and the Beautiful' (1952)
'Lust for Life' (1956)
'Spartacus' (1960)

SOPHIA LOREN

Sophia Loren's early life reads like a Hollywood weepy. The illegitimate daughter of a would-be actress, the young Sophia was put out to work as a model, in order to bring food to the table. The struggle was thankfully short-lived. Her extraordinary beauty and charm gave her work on screen - initially just in small parts - but it was only when producer Carlo Ponti came into her life, that her star began to truly rise. Ponti, who has continued to be instrumental in her life, came to ask the curvaceous Italian beauty to marry him in 1957, in spite of a twenty-two year age gap. Loren went on to win leads in 'The Pride and the Passion' (1957) and the delightful comedy 'Houseboat' (1958), both co-starring Cary Grant. Despite her obvious success, Sophia tried desperately to dispel the myth that she was just a mere sex-goddess. However, the majority of the roles she was given contradicted her better efforts. Director Vittorio de Sica came to her rescue casting her in 'Two Women' (1961), for which she won an Oscar. Next came 'El Cid' (1961) and then two more De Sica movies including 'Marriage Italian Style' (1964). During the 60s, she performed two duets with the comedian Peter Sellers - 'Goodness Gracious Me' and 'Bangers and Mash' - both of which were major hits in the British music charts. By the end of the decade, Loren's screen career had begun to wane. Theatre wasn't an option as she suffered from terrible stage fright. Undaunted, she bounced back during the late 70s with 'Cassandra Crossing' (1976) and 'Una Giornata Particolare' (1977). In 1982, she served an eighteen-day prison sentence in Italy for tax evasion. Ten years later, she and fellow actress Myrna Loy were awarded Honorary Oscars for their unique contribution to the cinema. A veteran of over 100 films, her most recent, 'Between Strangers' (2002) was directed by her son Edoardo Ponti.

Top Three Films:
'Houseboat' (1958)
'Marriage Italian Style' (1964)
'Sophia: Living and Loving' (1979)

BEAUTIFUL, FEISTY AND ITALIAN. SOPHIA LOREN BY FRANK WORTH

JEFF CHANDLER

The son of a Jewish silk-merchant, Jeff Chandler was born Ira Grossel in Brooklyn in 1918. After high school, he took a drama course and worked in stock companies for two years. His next role would be that of an officer in WWII. After he was discharged from service, Chandler busied himself, acting in radio dramas and comedies until he was eventually signed by Universal. It was the 1950s that saw Jeff become a true star, making westerns and action pictures. He was to be nominated for an Academy Award for his role as Cochise in 'Broken Arrow' (1950). Tall, rugged and with distinctive silver grey curly hair, he soon became a popular pin-up. Beyond being a very versatile actor, the multi-talented Chandler was also a singer, musician and songwriter who released a number of singles and albums in the 50s. Following MGM's lead, Universal dumped nearly all of its contract players at that time, although Chandler's strong appeal kept him working in front of the cameras. He also produced two of his films, 'Drango' (1957) and 'The Plunderers' (1960). Tragically, his career was cut short when aged 42, he died of blood poisoning following an operation for a slipped disc. Chandler's name became headline news some three decades after his death, when former lover, Esther Williams, revealed in her autobiography his alleged penchant for dressing in women's clothing. Needless to say, her revelations were angrily refuted by many of his adoring fans.

Top Three Films:
'Broken Arrow' (1950)
'Sign of the Pagan' (1954)
'Return to Peyton Place' (1961)

JEFF CHANDLER (L), JANET LEIGH, TONY CURTIS AND ROCK HUDSON (R) OUT ON THE TOWN

RITA HAYWORTH

'Rita hadn't quite yet made it when I did the big shoot with her. We were both kids back then, but she displayed the prowess of a star'.

Frank Worth
(1987)

RITA HAYWORTH, STILL A NEWCOMER IN HOLLYWOOD, STROLLS ALONG WILSHIRE BOULEVARD

FRANK SINATRA AND LAUREN BACALL

'I have no friends in Hollywood anymore. I miss my friends. Out of twenty I had, I'll miss the six I really have narrowed down in the passage of time, since Bogey's death. But I won't miss the idle chitchat, the smiling, simultaneous hello and goodbye, the meaningless blown kisses and meaningless conversations, the constant scrutiny of one's private life, including my relationships. I won't miss the constant comment that everything is great, no matter what. I won't miss having my head in the sand.'

Lauren Bacall
Films in Review
(1974)

FRANK SINATRA AND LAUREN BACALL DATED FOR A WHILE DURING THE LATE 1950s

IN COLOUR

RESTORATION

"Due to poor storage and the degradation of the original films, much of Frank Worth's damaged and faded colour work has been restored to it's former glory by using the latest digital technology.

Richard Hadley's painstaking work has ensured that these images are not an approximation of the true colour, but an accurate restoration using the colour information still embedded in the original transparencies and negatives.

What one can see here is exactly Frank Worth's view at the time these images were committed to film"

Nicholas Jordan
Managing Director
Cinemage Limited

DORIS DAY

Doris Day was without doubt the brightest star of the 1950s, earning many titles and nicknames during her career. The one that stuck was 'The Professional Virgin' - a result of the puritanical, morally upright ladies she usually portrayed. Far from being stiff or unadventurous, Day with her quaffed blonde hair, wholesome freckled complexion and sparkling blue eyes, was a favourite teenage pin-up. She had originally set out to become a dancer, but took a change of direction when injured in a car crash. Doris entered show business singing with the Bob Crosby and Les Brown orchestras. She appeared with Brown in a pair of 1941 musical shorts, but didn't make her first feature until 'Romance on the High Seas' (1948). It was not until 'Calamity Jane' (1953) that she broke free from Warner's sedate musicals to play the Wild West's leading tomboy - and it still remains her favourite part. She won the praise of audiences during the early 60s with a run of sophisticated but wholesome sex comedies opposite those all-American boys, Rock Hudson and James Garner. These assured her place in movie history. By the end of the 1970s, Day sought solace in looking after sick and injured animals. *"They don't answer back",* she said. *"Animals are incredibly loyal too"*. Her first three husbands viciously beat then deserted her, stripping her bank accounts. She has constantly resisted all offers to return to the screen. Largely reclusive today, Doris Day has ventured from her Carmel hideaway back to Hollywood just once, as a special guest of Clint Eastwood at the 64th Annual Academy Awards.

Top Three Films:
'Calamity Jane' (1953)
'Pillow Talk' (1959)
'Move Over Darling' (1963)

JAMES STEWART AND DORIS DAY AT MGM STUDIOS (1958)

NATALIE WOOD

'People always saw me as Natalie Wood, the child actor, the teenager, the rebel, but rarely did they realise I'd grown up. They never allowed me to do so. Subsequently I received hardly any scripts'.

Natalie Wood
(1979)

BRINGING OUT THE BEAST IN NATALIE WOOD

AUDREY HEPBURN AND REX HARRISON

FRANK SINATRA AND NATALIE WOOD

MAUREEN O'HARA, ED WYNN AND ZSA ZSA GABOR

GENE KELLY AND BETSY BLAIR

SNAPSHOTS: SOME OF HOLLYWOOD'S BIGGEST STARS AT THE PREMIERE OF 'MY FAIR LADY' (1964)

AVA GARDNER

'Ava was the most beautiful creature I had ever seen'

Frank Worth
(1987)

AVA GARDNER (1958)

BING CROSBY

Bing Crosby entered Gonzaga College, Spokane intent on becoming a lawyer. However, upon joining the college band it became clear that Crosby was destined for a career in music. He recorded his first album in 1926, entitled, 'I've Got the Girl', whilst simultaneously performing in an act called 'The Rhythm Boys' with the Paul Whiteman orchestra. Mack Sennett, who had brought Charlie Chaplin and Gloria Swanson to the screen, spotted Crosby at the famed Coconut Grove and signed him for 'I Surrender Dear' (1931) with Marion Sayers, followed by 'Billboard Girl' (1932). He was already an established radio star when Paramount Studio placed him in the all-star 'Big Broadcast of 1932'. He eventually went on to star in over fifty-five full-length features, notably alongside Bob Hope and Dorothy Lamour in the 'Road to...' series. At the time of his death in 1977, Crosby had been recognised as the world's most successful singer, in terms of record sales, recording more than 1,700 songs. His 1942 hit 'White Christmas' topped the charts in three different years and is still the most requested nostalgic Christmas Holiday tune on radio. On October 14 1977 and aged seventy-three, Crosby died of a massive heart attack whilst playing a game of his beloved golf in Spain. Both of his wives, Dixie Lee and Kathryn Grant, were actresses.

Top Three Films:
'Pennies From Heaven' (1936)
'Road to Singapore' (1940)
'A Connecticut Yankee in King Arthur's Court' (1949)

A GOOD READ? BING CROSBY'S NOT SO SURE!

JUDY GARLAND

The girl who followed the yellow brick road to the Emerald City in 'The Wizard of Oz' (1939) displayed a compulsive quality even during her first stage appearance at the bonny age of thirty months. Born Frances Gumm in 1922, Judy Garland came from a theatrical family in Grand Rapids, Minnesota. Her mother, Ethel, wished for Judy and her siblings to be in the movies and moved the entire family to California. As one of the 'Gumm Girls', Garland appeared at various shows, including the Chicago World's Fair in 1934. It soon became clear that the energetic, effervescent Judy was the focal point of the family act. Her big break came when 20th Century Fox refused to loan Shirley Temple to MGM for the title role of Dorothy Gale in 'The Wizard of Oz' (1939). She sang "Over the Rainbow", which became her signature tune, and won a special Academy Award in the process. Margaret Pellegrini who played one of the Munckins in the movie recalled, *'Judy was a sweet girl. She was a typical teenager and contrary to the wild rumours, she loved the Munckins'*. MGM mogul, Louis B Mayer kept tight control of his brightest acquisition, insuring she could perform by feeding her prescribed 'uppers' in the morning and 'downers' to put her to sleep. When the bright lights were switched on, Judy sparkled with wondrous effect but as they dimmed, so did her star. She dazzled her way through several 1940s musicals, worked with MGM's finest and in 1945, married director Vincente Minnelli. Their daughter Liza was born the following year. By 1950, Garland was becoming swamped by her professional career, attempting suicide in June of that year. In 1951, Garland divorced Minnelli and married producer Sidney Luft. He was instrumental in orchestrating her comeback, with a series of successful tours. She hosted her own television show during the early 60s, but by this time was once again reliant on drugs. She and Luft - who had two children together - Lorna and Joey, divorced in 1965. A year later she married and divorced the young actor Mark Heron and in March 1969, married Mickey Deans, a nightclub manager. Three months after, this irreplaceable legend died from an overdose.

Top Three Films:
'The Wizard of Oz' (1939)
'Meet Me in St. Louis' (1944)
'A Star is Born' (1954)

JUDY GARLAND (1954)

JUNE ALLYSON

June Allyson was advised to take ballet lessons following a serious childhood accident. An avid fan of Fred Astaire and Ginger Rogers musicals, she viewed them time and time again, desperate to emulate their grace and style. Adamant that she had what it took, Allyson arrived at auditions for a Broadway show and was subsequently signed to the chorus of 'Sing Out The News', a Rogers and Hart musical. Several other shows followed, including 'Best Foot Forward', choreographed by Gene Kelly. An MGM talent scout spotted her, resulting in a long-term contract to the studio. Allyson was publicised as a clean-cut all-American girl and put to work in a succession of films, including the light-romantic heroine in the film versions of 'Best Foot Forward' (1943) and 'Little Women' (1949) starring Elizabeth Taylor and Mary Astor. Within a relatively short space of time, she had become one of cinema audience's most adored actresses. For six consecutive years, Allyson was voted the Number One Box Office Attraction in America and was among the top ten favourite personalities in the picture industry for a solid ten-year spell. In 1959, she hosted her own immensely popular television show, produced by her then husband Dick Powell. But saccharine sweetness isn't always in vogue and hers went out of fashion. Undaunted, she returned to the stage and occasionally appeared in television commercials. In 1996, Allyson became the first recipient of the Harvey Award in recognition for her positive contribution to the world of entertainment. Resides in Ojai, California.

Top Three Films:
'Good News' (1947)
'Little Women' (1949)
'The Glenn Miller Story' (1953)

HUMPHREY BOGART INTERRUPTS FILMING TO CHAT WITH JUNE ALLYSON

SAMMY DAVIS JR.

The diminutive black performer Sammy Davis Jr. was hailed by many as the world's greatest living entertainer. He was a remarkably popular and versatile performer equally adept at acting, singing, dancing and impersonations. He had become a fully-fledged professional dancer by the age of four, having begun his show business career at the age of only eighteen months. At seven years old, Davis made his film debut in the legendary musical short 'Rufus Jones for President' (1933) and, later, received tap-dancing lessons from Bill 'Bojangles' Robinson. During the WWII, he worked entertaining the troops, although he endured a constant battle against racism. Upon his return, he re-joined his father and uncle in the 'Will Mastin Trio'. Eventually Davis made the break and began appearing on Broadway and releasing records. In 1954 he signed up with Decca, topping the charts with his debut album, 'Starring Sammy Davis Junior'. In the same year, he lost an eye in a much-publicized automobile accident. He recovered, and by 1958 was fulfilling his ambition to appear in the movies. Davis is probably best recognized by cinemagoers as one of the key members of the Las Vegas Rat Pack, a loose confederation of Frank Sinatra associates. In 1960, Sinatra, Davis, Peter Lawford and Joey Bishop teamed up to make 'Ocean's Eleven'. Davis continued to entertain globally until the late eighties. A heavy smoker, he died of cancer in 1990.

Top Three Films:
'Porgy and Bess' (1959)
'Ocean's Eleven' (1960)
'Robin and the Seven Hoods' (1964)

SAMMY DAVIS JR. JUMPS THE CITYSCAPE

AVA GARDNER

'I'm one movie star who hasn't tried to slash her wrists, take sleeping pills or kick a cop in the shins'.

Ava Gardner
The MGM Stock Company
(1973)

AVA GARDNER AT THE 1952 ANNUAL ACADEMY AWARDS

SELECTED BIBLIOGRAPHY

Ankerich, Michael G. *The Sound of Silence.* North Carolina: McFarland & Company, Inc. 1998

Barondess MacLean, Barbara. *One Life Is Not Enough.* New York: Future Press, 1986

Bellamy, Madge. *A Darling of the Twenties.* New York: Vestal Press, 1989

Broccoli, Barbara. *I Used To Be In Pictures.* London: Astoria Productions, 2000

Chekmayan, Ara. *Forever James Dean.* Time Warner Entertainment/Chelsea Communications, 1988

Davis, Bette, and Michael Herskowitz. *This 'n That.* London: Sidgwick & Jackson, 1987

Flamini, Ronald. *Thalberg: The Last Tycoon and the World of MGM.* New York: Crown Publishers, 1994

Griffith, Richard. *The Movie Stars.* New York: Doubleday & Co, 1970

Head, Edith, and Paddy Calistro. *Edith Head's Hollywood.* New York: E.P. Dutton, 1983

Hopper, Hedda. *From Under My Hat.* Garden City. New York: Doubleday & Co, 1952

Hobart, Rose. *A Steady Digression to a Fixed Point.* New Jersey: The Scarecrow Press, Inc., 1994

Kobal, John. *People Will Talk.* New York: Alfred A. Knopf, 1986

Lamparski, Richard. *Whatever Became of...?* New York: Crown Publishers, Inc., 1986

Lamparski, Richard. *Whatever Became of...?* New York: Crown Publishers, Inc., 1989

Lloyd, Ann, and Graham Fuller. *The Illustrated Who's Who of the Cinema.* London: Obis Publishing, 1983

Maltin, Leonard. *The Movie and Video Guide.* New York: Penguin/Putnum, Inc., 2001

McClelland, Doug. *Hollywood on Hollywood: Tinsletown Talks.* London: Faber & Faber, 1985

Parrish, Robert James. *The Hollywood Beauties.* New York: Arlington House Publishers, 1978

Paul, Michael. *Movie Greats.* London: Garland Books, 1969

Picturegoer's Who's Who and Encyclopedia, The. London: Oldham Press Ltd., 1932

Williams, Esther, and Digby Diehl. *The Million Dollar Mermaid.* London: Pocket Press, 1999

World Film Encyclopedia, The. - A Universal Screen Guide. London: Amalgamated Press, 1933

INDEX

* These images are available for purchase as Limited Edition Fine Art Prints.
Please visit www.frankworth.com or call on 0870 443 0800.
Those whose names appear in bold indicates a biography. The page on which the biography falls is in italics.

"For us Frank Worth was a man with a big heart and an even bigger bag of movie star dreams he lived out till the day he died... probably all alone and unattended."

Marty Ingels and Shirley Jones
(2002)

CW01582557

This book belongs to. . .

For Sam, Nathan and Charlotte
H.H.

To Jason for all his love and support,
thanks to you I also can
N.A.

ORCHARD BOOKS
First published in Great Britain in 2023
by Hodder & Stoughton
10 9 8 7 6 5 4 3 2 1

Text © Hollie Hughes, 2023
Illustrations © Nila Aye, 2023

The moral rights of the author and
illustrator have been asserted.
All rights reserved.

A CIP catalogue record for this book
is available from the British Library.

HB ISBN 978 1 40836 718 6
PB ISBN 978 1 40836 719 3

Printed and bound in China

FSC www.fsc.org MIX Paper from responsible sources FSC® C104740

Orchard Books
An imprint of Hachette Children's Group
Part of Hodder & Stoughton
Carmelite House, 50 Victoria Embankment,
London EC4Y 0DZ

An Hachette UK Company
www.hachette.co.uk
www.hachettechildrens.co.uk

little bugs **BIG FEELINGS**

You Can Do It, Clover!

Hollie Hughes Nila Aye

ORCHARD

In the wild patch of the garden,
under brambles roaming free,
live little bugs whose feelings
are as **big** as **big can be**.

Come, step inside this story,
for the tale will lead the way,
to **Clover Caterpillar**,
who we'll meet out there today.

A happy caterpillar,
on the outside and within,
who wouldn't change a smidge about
the skin that she is in.

Little Clover's days are filled
with all she loves to do
and, in her life of joy and fun,
her worries are but few.

But caterpillars come upon
a time when they must sleep,
and awaken as a butterfly,
their childhood days complete . . .

. . . ready to take flight and join

The Flutterby Parade,

where every flying bug shows off

the progress they have made.

Clover's scared of changing though –
she'd rather hide away,
and stay the way she's always been,
the way she is today.

"Come on," calls her friend Basil,
"you've not even tried it yet.
I'll take you butterflying –
it's the most fun you can get."

"But I'll miss cabbage," Clover says,
"and the burrows I love best.

And I don't think I could
balance on a flower
head to rest.

I'm so truly scared of flying,
and fluttering in the air,

and my Caterpillar Shuffle skills
might float away up there!"

"Don't fret," says Basil kindly,
"come with me to Queen Bee's Teas."
Then together they munch cabbage,
and sip nectar – freshly squeezed!

"Now climb aboard, and you will get
a butterfly's-eye view.
You can do it, Clover –
you can change, like I did too."

At first they take off slowly,
waving to their friends below,
but soon they're flying faster,
whooping loudly as they go.

They visit Buddy Bee to help
fetch pollen from the flowers,
and race past Laurel Ladybird,
with acrobatic powers.

They glide onto a bluebell,
swaying gently in the breeze,
and Clover finds she's balancing
with unexpected ease.

Then Basil flies up high,
to his burrow in a tree,
and Clover cannot help admit
it's cosy as can be.

With one final step to take,
Basil boogies into line,
to prove he's still got moves –
it's Caterpillar Shuffle time!

Clover leads the dance,
followed closely by her friends.
Change, she starts to realise,
doesn't mean the party ends!

"Thank you, Basil," Clover yawns,
"you've helped me on my way.

Butterfly life might just be fun –
a new start from today."

Then she curls up tightly snug,
drifting dreamy deep asleep.

And, when she wakes . . .

. . . her wings have grown –

her change is now complete!

Clover finds it's not as scary
as she thought that it would be.

“Change is not so bad,” she laughs,
“it’s turned me into **ME**.”

Then Clover flies with Basil,
in **The Flutterby Parade**,
as the other bugs all celebrate
the progress they have made.

And one thing that will never change,
or ever reach an end,
is the fun they each have found
in the other as a friend.

But it's time to say goodbye,
to the bug we've met today –
to **Clover BUTTERFLY**,
whose true story led the way.

We'll be back to visit soon, this
whole world beneath our feet,
and the **most amazing creatures**
we could ever wish to meet.